Primer for
Small Systems
Management

WINTHROP COMPUTER SYSTEMS SERIES

Gerald M. Weinberg, *editor*

COATS AND PARKIN
Computer Models in the Social Sciences

CONWAY AND GRIES
Primer on Structural Programming Using PL/I, PL/C, and PL/CT

CONWAY, GRIES, AND WORTMAN
Introduction to Structured Programming Using PL/I and SP/k

CONWAY, GRIES, AND ZIMMERMAN
A Primer on PASCAL

CONWAY
A Primer on Disciplined Programming Using PL/I, PL/CS, and PL/CT

EASLEY
Primer for Small Systems Management

FINKENAUR
COBOL for Students: A Programming Primer

GELLER AND FREEDMAN
Structured Programming in APL

GILB
Software Metrics

GILB AND WEINBERG
Humanized Input: Techniques for Reliable Keyed Input

WEINBERG, WRIGHT, GOETZ, AND KAUFFMAN
High Level COBOL Programming

FUTURE TITLES

CRIPPS
Computer Hardware

ECKHOUSE AND SPIER
Guide to Programming

GREENFIELD
The Architecture of Microcomputers

LINES
Minicomputer Systems

POOCH
Simulation

SHNEIDERMAN
Human Factors in Computer and Information Systems

TOPPING
Simula Programming

WILCOX
Introduction to Compiler Construction

(continued from front flap)

ABOUT THE AUTHOR

G. M. Easley is Director of Data Processing and Assistant Secretary of Rice Food Markets, Inc. A graduate of the University of Texas at Austin, Mr. Easley has nearly thirty years' experience in small system accounts, equipment conversions, and new installations—from the earliest unit records through the IBM 360, the System 3 in its several configurations, and the 370 line, including on-line systems and limited tele- communications. He has served as Director of the Data Processing Management Asso- ciation and in 1974 was the recipient of that organization's Individual Performance Award. He is also an organizing member of and program speaker for the Houston Asso- ciation of System 3 Users.

Primer for Small Systems Management

Grady M. Easley

Director of Data Processing
Assistant Secretary
Rice Food Markets, Inc.

Winthrop Publishers, Inc.
Cambridge, Massachusetts

Library of Congress Cataloging in Publication Data

Easley, Grady M   *03999/*
    Primer for small systems management.

    (Winthrop computer systems series)
    Bibliography: p. 157
    Includes index.
    1.   Electronic data processing departments—
Management.   I.   Title.
HF5548.2.E22   658'.05'4   77-26824
ISBN 0-87626-716-9

Jacket design by Harold Pattek

*HF
5548.2
.E22
1978*

Jacket graphic by Roger Vilder
from the series *Variations with 9 Squares (1971)*
Courtesy of Galerie Gilles Gheerbrant, Montreal

© 1978 by Winthrop Publishers, Inc.
    17 Dunster Street, Cambridge, Massachusetts 02138

10 9 8 7 6 5 4 3 2 1

for

P. E. L.

"why are you doing it that way?"

Contents

Foreword

Perhaps it is surpassed by Alpine sheepherding or traversing the Pacific in a dinghy, but for my money, managing a small data processing system must be the world's loneliest job. By taking responsibility for the lion's share of the informational needs of a small organization, the systems manager moves into a world where none of the dozens of people encountered each day can share that curiously unique set of problems. The manager learns a new language and thereby becomes isolated from the ordinary people in the business, yet he doesn't learn the language well enough to commune with the flock of computer specialists that troop through the place like—well, like Alpine sheep. Somewhere, outside of these glass and aluminum walls, there must be other small systems managers who could understand both the language and the problems—but, then, the manager is far too busy to leave these walls for more than a quick meal, a few hours of sleep, and perhaps an occasional visit with the family.

It's truly hard to think of another job that makes such demands on a person. There is no such thing as sacrosanct personal time, for any hour of the day or night may require the manager to stop the buck and start the system. There is no such thing as an irrelevant fact, for any isolated piece of information about the hardware, the software, the application, the people, the law, or just about anything at all can be the key that unlocks the puzzle that stands between loss and profit. Other people in the organization can specialize, leaving great holes in their knowledge of the business, but the systems manager must add a rather complete general knowledge to a most demanding menu of data processing information. It's only on rare occasions, then, that small systems managers find time to go out into the world and seek companionship with their own kind. Sometimes I meet one of them at a meeting of the ASM, DPMA, or ACM where I've been invited to speak. Usually, they complain that the program committee consists of employees of large corporations—specialists who would be carried off in straitjackets after twenty-four hours of trying to hold down the small systems fort.

"Then why do you come to these meetings?" I ask.

"Well, I thought I might meet someone else who's in the same situation, so we might exchange notes."

Fortunately, things are improving for the lonely small systems manager. Here and there we find a really active chapter of a group or subgroup specializing in the problems of the small system. A few magazines have passed a critical circulation level and may survive to bring the small systems manager some friendly greetings once every month or two. And now, in *Primer for Small Systems Management*, the small system manager has a desk-top companion to turn to in his loneliest hour.

Grady Easley's book is really like a companion. To quote the author himself, "Most of it is personal experience and knowledge acquired through the years." And not, I might add, a lot of vague, theoretical bunk accumulated from dusty textbooks. When you pick up the *Primer* and turn to any subject, you feel as if you're having a discussion with a colleague. It's a discussion based on genuine experience, communicated with every effort to make it clear, interesting, and useful to other small systems managers.

Some years ago, I managed what today would be a small system. It was expensive then, but it was subsidized, so the situation was very similar to that facing today's manager. If anyone had a problem with an existing system, or wanted to solve some problem with a future system, I was *it*. After over a year of this struggle, I happened to meet the manager of an almost identical installation four hours away. We talked endlessly, exchanging an incredible amount of useful information ranging over more or less the same topics covered in this book. We found, in the end, that time after time we had solved the same problem, independently, sometimes with great trials and tribulations. In examining *Primer for Small Systems Management* for inclusion in the Winthrop Computer Systems Series, I recalled many of those problems and asked myself if a copy of the book would have saved me grief. Again and again, the answer was yes. I find it hard to imagine a small systems manager anywhere in the world who won't find similar answers in every chapter.

Of course with a book as personal as this *Primer*, everyone will find a few things to argue about. So much the better, I say, for only by wrestling with conflicting approaches do we build our mental muscles and develop the skills the small systems manager needs every day. Unlike the ordinary textbook, the *Primer* takes a down-to-earth factual approach that keeps the reader on the plane of the author's *colleague*, which encourages him to wrestle with the ideas personally.

These same qualities make *Primer for Small Systems Management* a most fortuitous choice as a textbook in, say, a community or junior college. Because it deals with the real problems encountered by a real person in a real organization, the *Primer* draws the student out of the rarefied atmosphere of the classroom and brings him into the excitement of today's world of information processing. It would make a terrific present for any young person considering a career in data processing—I don't know of any other that gives the same complete view while conveying the on-the-scene richness and vitality.

I suspect that instructors who use *Primer for Small Systems Management* as a text—in, say, an Introduction to Data Processing course—will find the students raising lots of interesting questions, coming up with numerous ideas of their own, and almost demanding to be taken on a field trip to some small data processing installation. I hope that's true, and I hope that the instructor will be wise enough to take them to such a place, rather than to some giant installation where the forest of data processing is lost among the trees of specialization. I hope so for their sakes, for the instructor's sake, but most of all for the sake of the lonely system manager—who would love nothing more than a chance to talk to someone who might really *understand* what it's like.

But until that visit, I think that it will be comforting to have Grady Easley visiting whenever you need him.

Gerald M. Weinberg

Preface

The specialized skills so essential for the successful management of a small data processing installation can be acquired by trial and error over a period of months and years. However, today's business environment does not allow the luxury of experimentation. As a contributing member of a management team or group, your decisions must be sure and effective. This brief, succinct primer is written to assist the new manager and/or programmer in developing an awareness of the multitudinous tasks facing a new supervisor in the small- to medium-sized installation.

Most, if not all, of the available data processing literature is written and directed toward the enhancement of programming skills and techniques. Other articles in trade publications are devoted to discussions of abstruse subjects that are of limited value or use in the small shop. As a result, for example, data base systems are only slowly being adapted for use on the System 3. Indeed, many large-scale users consider the System 3 suitable only for use as a remote job entry (RJE) terminal, with communications being controlled by the host system. This is not the case. The System 3 is a powerful, compact system entirely capable of meeting the needs of a multimillion-dollar corporation. This book is designed to aid in the refinement of those supervisory skills needed in the day-to-day administration and management of a (small) computer complex.

The newly promoted manager may be more than a little unaware of the many complexities involved in supervising an installation. The new position includes many assignments and tasks not adequately covered, nor even mentioned, in the job description. The duties are numerous, varied, and can be very demanding. Technical skills required for production programming will become of less importance as managerial skills increase. The emphasis will shift from purely technical matters to the personal challenges of displaying traits of managerial competence in making profitable and effective use of the System 3. A manager must have adroit skills in acquiring a grasp of budgets, planning, interpersonal relationships, interfacing with user departments, and communicating with other department heads. This book is designed to aid the newly appointed manager in developing all latent qualities of leadership. Job pressures are significantly more intense in the managerial chair. Effectiveness is measured, not only in actual production, but in all facets of corporate life. The task is not an easy one. The benefits—tangible and intangible—are personally and financially rewarding.

For the ambitious programmer who is anxious to earn the opportunity to manage an installation, this book offers suggestions and hints for developing a personal management philosophy. With the guidelines and recommendations described herein, a programmer can quickly learn, and adapt, by observation and practice. When the time comes for promotion and advancement, application of these principles will ease the transition into a management position. The skilled programmer, through observation and technique adaptation, will find this compendium of experiences to be of inestimable value in defining and refining those talents required for a supervisory position.

Portions of this book discuss the functional position of an installation; others discuss the need for internal and external controls. Still others discuss the relationships with user departments and personnel. Each chapter is written so that it will provide the young manager with an understanding of the many problems facing a supervisor.

In my career, I have been blessed with the advice and support of innumerable people. For my part, I have endeavored to repay the favors by helping and encouraging others to become successful managers. Those who have contributed particularly over the past few years include:

Leonard Piotrowski, IBM-GSD, Customer Engineer

Bob Doremus, IBM-DPD, Senior Marketing Representative

Jim Thomas, IBM-GSD, Senior Marketing Representative

Charlie Vyvial, IBM-GSD, Systems Representative, Houston

Bill Thompson, Co-owner and Manager, Control Forms, Inc., Houston

Particular thanks and acknowledgement must go to Ms. Anita McNamee, business education teacher for the Houston Independent School District, who made so many helpful (and needed) suggestions during manuscript preparation.

For the many contributions from an ex-IBM SE, my wife Penny, I can only say humbly—thank you. Without her encouragement, this book would have remained only a dream.

G.M.E.

Author's Comments

Since 1947, I have been observing the activities of supervisors, controllers, machine and data entry operators, corporate executives, and others as they approached the problems of managing a data processing installation. This work experience extends from the dying days of the IBM 405 through and including the System 3 and 370 series. In pushing cards and wiring control panels, there was much opportunity to think and sort out the possibilities of becoming an installation manager. As a career and profession, data processing seemed to offer the attractive combination of a portable occupation, daily challenges, and an opportunity to prove skills as an effective manager. This had been the situation since that first day.

My first job in installation management presented supervisory problems that had not been mentioned in any of my college textbooks. Personnel, systems, and equipment problems presented an overwhelming number of "challenges and opportunities." Fortunately, my decisions were better than those of my predecessor, and I began to wonder about the long-range possibilities for data processing management.

Since that time, the methods and techniques for managing an installation have been my prime interest and concern. Instead of devoting energies to becoming a master programmer or systems analyst, I have concentrated on total aspects of data processing—corporate matters, staffing, general management, controlling, and assembling a competent staff. This interest in and concern for the entire process of management has been exciting and rewarding. The excitement has been partially in the gathering of management experience. Basic principles of management have been of much benefit in general application, but lack specifics for data processing supervision.

By participating in organized data processing groups (DPMA and the Houston Association of System 3 users), I discovered that many young new managers were trying to manage on the basis of technical competence and had little knowledge of or exposure to the process of management. This lack of experience has delayed acceptance of data processing in many corporations. This delay is directly traceable to a manager's lack of knowledge concerning duties and responsibilities of an installation manager. This book is designed to provide a smoother path for the student of data processing and those new managers who are in their first supervisory position.

In these limited pages, I have tried to mention those major tasks and assignments which are vital to the manager. It is not possible to include every facet of experience in one book. For those students who say, "But what about..." they are entirely correct. The purpose of this book is to provide a primer—not an encyclopedia.

Primer for
Small Systems
Management

chapter 1

Introduction to Data Processing

Commercial data processing can be, should be, and is the key to success for the corporate enterprise of today. The computer, in its many forms, provides the tool (information) on which to make intelligent, well-informed decisions. Any manager worth his salt will be able to make intelligent decisions that spell success for a particular organization. One key to good decision-making is the information used in reaching an actual decision.

Computer power can be used to reduce the information-gathering phase. The computer can also decrease time required for organizing and assimilating this information. The power of the computer can be used to make presentation of data more pleasing to the eye, and more importantly, logical and complete. However, ultimate decisions can only rest in the hands of the manager. This decision-making process—go or no-go—cannot be delegated to, nor vested in, the computer. A manager is responsible for defining the parameters of a problem. It is just as logical to program a computer to function within these boundaries. However, the final decision remains, and must remain, vested in the manager. This means effective decision-making should be based on managerial intelligence *and* all available information.

When Christopher Columbus embarked upon his journey, he had a goal, a budget based on proceeds from mortgaged jewelry, and a vision of future rewards. Based on then unknowns in this situation, it is doubtful that Queen Isabella made an "intelligent, well-informed decision." Based on our knowledge of events since 1492, she did a magnificent job of making the best possible decision at the time, based on available facts.

Entrepreneurs of today are faced with much the same problem as our Queen Isabella. Prospects of profit are present, information is available somewhere; and there are tools (the computer) to be used in bringing these prospects into reality. Business data processing is the path to making reality out of what were once just prospects for success.

As the manager of a data processing installation, you have the tools for bringing these nebulous plans into fruition. The prospects for your success are as vitally important as the goals and aspirations of the business owner–operator. It is your job, your reason for employment, your chance for successful enterprise.

With your available electronic equipment, one of your prime functions is to provide information leading to enhanced profits. Technical programming skills are not to be ignored. For a computer to function effectively, you must possess substantially more than a modicum of knowledge about the inner workings and structures of programs and files. Your success will be judged, overall, on contributions to profit and technical skills as they relate to electronic data processing.

Management cannot be expected to be overly concerned about bits, bytes, or blocking factors. That is your problem. Management is concerned with the "bottom line." Your job is to utilize resources to maximize impact on the bottom line of profits. For you to have a noticeable effect upon profits, you must make a contribution through effective utilization of your resources—manpower, money, and machines. To understand the background for these resources, we should examine the basic, underlying philosophy and reasons for a commercial data processing installation.

When you write a personal check in payment of your utility bill, you are actually engaged in a rudimentary form of data processing. This basic example ultimately becomes the justification for a computer installation. The labor involved in matching the bill with your checkbook, time spent in verifying the due date and amount, searching for the correct mailing address, entering date paid on the check and stub, writing the amount and signing the check is lost forever. This makes no allowance for later time to be spent in reconciling your personal bank account. If your time is worth $10 per hour (to your employer), and preparation of this one check took six minutes (total), then you have written a check for a relative cost of one dollar. Can you afford to pay for that one-time event? Obviously, you can and do.

We should examine the other side of the coin—the utility company. The utility company, at a high original unit cost, stored much of this same information in a computer. Repetitive operations such as billing, address lookup, due date and late penalty charges are all called forth when needed, prepared on high-speed printers, and so forth, at a cost far below the unit cost of personally writing a check. The result is a lower unit cost (for the utility) per utility bill—a unit cost much lower than your own cost in paying amounts due. This simple example of cost effectiveness reflects two extremes—no automation, and one of highly sophisticated automation.

A small computer installation possesses many capabilities, if not the capacity for a high degree of sophisticated automation. Automation possibilities for the small shop are quickly noticeable and apparent in the reduction of clerical expenses as reflected in lower unit transaction costs, measurable time savings, and more profitable financial and operating statements. "Hard" savings are a quick means of ready justification for the machine—and yourself. "Hard" savings represent a measurement of actual cost reduction. Soft savings may only be estimated; they are potential savings that are only projections. Soft savings cannot be deposited in a bank account. If your computer installation is to become an integral part of management, you cannot rest on laurels derived from automation. Other profitable benefits are to be subsequently realized in information processing and providing of accurate, reliable management information in a timely manner.

Regardless of the value of information, your job does not end with delivery of finished reports. You must be prepared to sell the information. Management personnel, though they may possess skills and intuition for running a corporation, do not always understand and relate to the use of computerized information. For example, statistical Equal Employment Opportunity Commission analyses may indicate a high (or low) compliance with federal guidelines, but management may choose to regard these studies as additional personnel statistics which appear to be of little value. Sales reports prepared in a varying sequence, low-to-high or high-to-low, may indicate who are "high-rollers" and conversely, those who are "dogging" it. Frequently, management pays too much attention to positive aspects of the business, and too little to the negative aspects. It is your responsibility to point out potential uses for this information, and make intelligent suggestions for remedial actions to be taken. (More of this will be covered in Chapter 11.)

To manage the data processing function, you should possess more than a fair amount of knowledge about business operations in general, and specifically, your industry. The effect of data processing pervades and permeates the entire corporation. Whether the title of "Mr. DP" is used nicely, or in an unkind fashion, you will be responding to the title. Wear your title proudly.

You represent "the computer" to your employer. It is your job, and opportunity, to turn an electronic number-cruncher into a marvelous machine respected at all company levels. You cannot achieve this status if you know little about the internal workings of various departments and divisions. By knowing more, you contribute more to the organization in its entirety. For example, automating a payroll is one thing—if the checks are computed correctly. On the other hand, an incorrect payroll check raises questions and doubts covering the entire payroll. To be knowledgeable about departments and employees, you must get involved with the total picture of department functions. This you do by becoming involved with the corporation as a whole.

Subject to company goals and objectives, it becomes your responsibility as data processing manager to set your professional goals in line with the company in reaching these objectives. In many instances these two sets of goals will be moving toward a common point. Your plans and efforts will be an integral part of the company's plan for success. Many years ago, while doing a stint in the U.S. Army, a group of basic trainees was posed the question, "What is the mission of the U.S. Army?" The recruits were young and dumb, requiring some prompting to respond with a stock answer—success in combat. Likewise, the free marketplace can be reasonably compared to a situation of struggle. The entrepreneur is attempting to secure a comfortable market niche at the expense of competition. To achieve this objective, the owner–operator must marshal many resources, strategically deploying them for maximum effect. The data processing installation can be the most powerful resource readily available and you are in charge of it. This is your responsibility—to use this resource wisely.

The common resources of business enterprises are personnel, machines, a product or service, and, of course, capital. Personnel can be hired and fired. Machines become obsolete because of changing technology, or simply by wearing out. Likewise, a product or service can become obsolete, or the market for it can disappear. As an example of product obsolescence, there is practically no demand in today's marketplace for buggywhips or isinglass curtains.

Capital does not become obsolete. It may be wasted or squandered, but never made obsolete. Capital may be hidden away, it may be put in a safe place—where growth is stifled—or it may be invested wisely with certain elements of acceptable risk. Your data processing installation is, or should be, an effective melding together of resources—personnel, money, and equipment with the idea of maximizing return on investment. Your challenge (and opportunity) is to maximize the usage of management information available through electronic data processing.

Over the last several years, as data processing has proven itself to the corporation, just as the cost-accountants did so many years ago, we have seen nomenclature change as the industry has grown in sophistication. Spanning the last two to three decades, "generations" of machine accounting equipment have come and gone—with almost visible rapidity. "Tab" shops were replaced with vacuum tubes, electro-mechanical relays, and rotating magnetic drums. With the advent of transistors, the generic term of data processing was applied to the computer field. Other terms— integrated data processing, management information systems, to name two—have surfaced, and one of the more acceptable terms of today is information processing.

This term rather effectively applies data processing to fill the gamut of enterprises, including government installations, military computers, nonprofit ventures, and of course to the commercial shop in profit-making enterprises. Data processing further implies electronic handling of numbers, formulae, and statistical data. Information processing is a "warmer" term; indicating information to be a living organism of constantly changing shapes and sizes.

Information Concepts

With this information concept in mind, you should take a critical, careful examination of the DP installation under your control. There are certain finite limitations to the amount of information that can be stored in a computer at any instant in time. Magnetic media (tape and disk) are removable and expand absolute capacity to an almost infinite degree.

In a world of budgets and limited storage space, there is a finite limit to the amount of available information stored on- or off-line. Another inernal limitation is the amount of core memeory available for processing data. This also leads to a maximum available configuration. These built-in physical limitations place certain restrictions on the amounts of information readily available at any instant in time.

A manager will want all available information before making a decision. The art of decision-making rests on the ability of the manager to consider probabilities, use judgment, and pick a course leading toward success. The information, which you supply through the computer, must be accurate, timely, and comprehensive.

Information can be, and is, compared to a perishable commodity. A tomato in the supermarket is not good once it has begun to rot. An empty seat on an airline has perished (certainly for one leg of the journey) the instant a plane is airborne. Information must be carefully selected, nurtured, and managed through its life cycle. It is your responsibility to constantly stay alert for the condition of computer-supplied information. Information needed for any business enterprise must be carefully weighed, evaluated, and rejected in some instances, before inclusion in the system.

The entrepreneurial manager has a problem in deciding what to do with available information. The DP manager has a similar problem. A DP manager must consider available options (core, disk, tape, etc.) to make data processing decisions for meeting the stated needs of management. The *effective* DP manager will meet not only stated needs, but will make necessary plans enabling the computer installation to adjust rapidly for a changing environment.

This is information planning for the future—where your shop will be tomorrow. It not only provides management with today's needs; it provides opportunity for anticipating the future. Planning for the future may insure the success of information processing in your shop. Consider the following cases:

Situation 1. The personnel master payroll file for your company contains the following information: (1) surname; (2) initials; (3) date of birth; (4) hire date; (5) mailing address; (6) job assignment; (7) full-time/part-time status; (8) department assignment; (9) rate of pay; (10) tax status.

Situation 2. Traditional sales analyses for your firm have only included the following: (1) salesman number; (2) dollar sales; (3) sales by customer; (4) departmental sales; (5) monthly sales and year to date.

These two simplistic examples are totally out of phase with reality. Situation one completely ignores race, sex, union affiliation, marital status, and a myriad of other items. In the second situation, no mention was made of number of sales transactions, gross profit on departmental sales, gross profit contribution by customer, customer returns, or sales by product or product line. With this information, no one could make an intelligent decision.

Situations like this develop when information is allowed to perish. To manage effectively, with the aid and assistance of computer-generated and supplied information, information must be as inclusive as the situation allows. In the cases described above, it is not sufficient to have supplied the user with requested information. It is a function of DP to meet and exceed—when and where possible—requests from the user departments. It is also a function of the information system to supply undefined needs. Obviously, there are more needs for information than what is indicated in the two examples. Supplying additional data is the first step toward doing an effective job of information management.

Information, whether supplied through your shop or gathered from other sources, must be marketed. Responsibility for preparing and presenting this information does not rest solely with the DP manager. The integrity of information actually begins with the salesman dictating information into his tape recorder, or with the shop supervisor scribbling numbers on a document at a work station along the production line. The actual proof of the information is the finished product that is presented to management. Regardless of the myriad sources and number of hands that information has passed through, the computer-prepared report carries with it the professional integrity of the manufacturer, your subordinates, and the imprimatur of your professional production standards. In the final analysis, the finished product will bear your signature in big capital letters. For information to be meaningful, it must be prepared with the end-user in mind; i.e., it must be accurate, timely, and complete.

Marketing of this information may be described as explaining, presenting, and justifying the report. (I know of a DP manager in a wholesale firm who managed to get a company sales commission plan revised by carefully preparing and presenting a statistical report on dollar sales volume *and* gross profit by number of transactions. The man made no friends among the sales force, but he managed to focus on inequities in the original plan which was based solely on dollar volume.) In this simple portrayal of effectively used computing power, this DP manager was able to increase company gross profits and increase salesman productivity. This was a relatively new concept at the time and would have failed miserably if the DP manager had not made an excellent presentation with valid information. The package—timeliness, accuracy, and effective marketing—provided the sales manager with the opportunity to manage with better information.

Inherent difficulties with information management can exist. Problems arise with the flow of information requests, information coming *down* from management, accepted verbatim by the DP shop. Management, once tasting sweet success with the use of computerized information, may develop what appears to be an insatiable demand for more information. There is information occupying large spaces within a system and then there is productive information.

It is your duty as a manager to manipulate computer resources to maintain only those materials which can be utilized for maximizing profits. Blind, unquestioning obedience and compliance with useless information requests will only fill files with the odor of rotting vegetables. Your responsibility does not end with request fulfillment; it is only beginning. Certain unavoidable costs are involved in recording and storing of data. Given any options at all, most managers will ask for all available information. Never mind that some information is not functionally necessary; 'tis better to have it and not need it than to need it and not have it. If there is any reasonable doubt, data should be included; but only after possible uses have been measured, evaluated and considered. This raises the question of needs versus wants.

Needs versus Wants

You may, and should, look up the various meanings of "needs" and "wants" in a good dictionary. The meanings are quite different, and there are many gradations between the two simple nouns. An identical situation exists with information. A DP manager is charged with satisfying "needs and wants" and responsibility for recognizing the difference.

Needed information is absolutely vital to every program, process, and procedure in data processing. It would be incomprehensible to have a payroll without an employee number of some sort—be it an assigned set of digits, a structured code involving department and location, the last six digits of Social Security number, or a combination of letters and digits. Major items will be dictated by needs of the application and company. The process of decision-making concerning the merit of facts to be included is simple. First, the nature of an application may dictate need; and second, it is easy to include this material by default. Future planning may indicate a need for a field of information. It is a simple decision to include items without discussion. It would be a wise conclusion to allocate space if there is some legitimate question as to real need for the future. If the facts are only "nice to have," then you may reserve space (this is good planning) but elect not to save the entries for the time being. This information could clutter the files, add to cost of maintenance, and have little redeeming value. A need, be it file, field, or record, should be examined on the basis of merit. This may not hold true when addressing "wants."

A "want" may be classified in any one of several categories:

1. Nice to have.
2. We *may* need these facts someday.
3. I want all available information stored at all times.
4. I *might* need this at year's end, next year, or sometime in the future.

These examples indicate only potentially negative aspects of want satisfaction, but all wants are not negative in nature. Some items are needed only once a year, and the value received may more than offset expenses of recording and storing. In many instances, the inclusion of wanted facts after reasonable justification becomes a computer asset. However, there is one valid reason for including wanted data in a file. Inclusion of specified facts and fields may *decrease* response time in the future and reduce data gathering requirements. This would be represented by information that may be used in the preparation of several reports.

The multiple usage, or processing, of data is most representative of effective computer processing. Costs of recording this information are spread over many applications, as are storage costs. In the days of unit-record equipment, there was a common axiom: A punched card used only once is too expensive to be used at all. This concept is still valid in considering data for recording and storage on magnetic media. Satisfying the "wants" of management may be one of the most difficult portions of your job. At the same time, careful planning may result in tightly defined systems that will satisfy "wants and needs" of your management.

An information system is a living organism changing its shape to meet shifting requirements. A computer provides you with the capabilities and power to react in a constantly evolving situation.

Review Questions

1.   Using the concept of wants and needs, list 10 items (personal) that you would classify as needs. Do the same for wants.

2.   Why is a record processed only once considered to be expensive?

3.   Define "intelligent, well-informed decisions."

4.   In any of the following environments, list instances wherein an employee number could be used repetitively:

(a) sales analysis

(b) machine shop production

(c) student accounting

(d) medical clinic (dental)

chapter 2

In-house
Computer
Facility

In accepting the job of managing a small computer installation, your management has elected to use an in-house computer. Financially, this decision could have far-reaching impact on the corporation. On a personal basis, success or failure of this installation will depend on the efforts and decisions you will be making as a manager. In this section of the chapter, we will consider the many opcions and choices available in managing the data processing facility.

In a new facility, a sales representative for the equipment vendor has studied the data processing requirements of the company. The degree of accuracy resulting from this study will be determined by a combination of the following:

1. Actual need for in-house computing power.
2. Money available to pay for "1" above.
3. Additional applications to justify added expense of equipment.
4. Costs for outside data processing services.
5. Other intangible costs.

If the installation of proposed equipment is to be successful, then a need for DP management has been established. The amount of required expertise may be somewhat dependent upon applications and configurations, but DP functions do not change. Your function as a DP supervisor is to carefully husband talents placed under your direction and supervision.

An in-house facility presents many opportunities to the resident manager. Whereas other available computing services are measured on a profit-making basis, the in-house shop does not follow the same costing rules. Or does it? The options for pure profit may not be present, but any business expenditure is expected, as a minimum, to pay its own way and provide other fiscal relief in the scheme of things.

Management of any enterprise is concerned with return on investment, and the computer room is no exception. If an installation does not earn its keep, management would do well to consider investing in certificates of deposit. You have the opportunity as DP director to provide the vendor-promised information and reports and accomplish this with a visible reduction of clerical costs. Your real achievement will be to provide those additional services which promise an even higher rate of return.

As a contributing member of management, you have certain duties and responsibilities. One is to preside over your resources—the DP installation—making it into a reliable source of facts for decision-making. This means your decisions will be judged and measured against corporate standards (do it right, and your job is safe). To make good decisions, you should consider all available sources of data. Some DP managers tend to regard outside sources as an erosion of their capabilities, but this is not the case. It affords you the chance to expand your services with comparatively small investments of time and money.

Even though you manage an in-house computer facility, you should be very aware of the powerful options that may be utilized to fulfill specific needs. Additional computing power may be used for overloads, peak load capacity, or limited one-time use of a powerful complex. The more common services are listed below:

1. Service bureaus.
2. Time-sharing terminals.
3. Remote job entry devices.
4. Combinations of the above.

These services are filling a real need. Different types of arrangements may be negotiated by shift, time of day, the hour, and just about any other measurable arrangement. The extra powers of a service organization must be considered in planning for your internal needs. These services can be used to fill certain technical needs on a one-time, or infrequent basis. In some instances, you may need a tremendous amount of computer power—for five to ten minutes per week. It would not be cost-effective to have this power in-house and utilized only one or two hours per month. (Remember the earlier examples of transaction unit costs.) Outside services can be arranged in many combinations, but we will examine each on a stand-alone basis.

Service Bureaus

The early service bureaus consisted of unit-record equipment, key-punches, verifiers, sorters, etc., supplying technical expertise to process certain fairly standard applications. There existed a real need for this service, and profits were to be made through significant "card-pushing" and long runs on the "tabulator." As the industry and economy grew, equipment also shifted to meet additional requirements of business.

Many small service operations sprang up overnight, operating on discounted time purchased at off-shift prices with a "moonlight" programmer/operator/manager/salesman. Many perished due to poor or non-existent business acumen. Others weathered the financial fallout, growing into substantial enterprises. Efficient service operations will have excellent equipment, a competent, well-trained staff, and the capabilities of providing specialized data processing. Some of the finest talent in the data processing industry may be found in a service bureau.

Arrangements that may be negotiated with a service bureau are limited only by skills of the two parties, but most agreements can be summarized into the following major headings:

1. Time and materials.
2. Shift, prime time, or less expensive hours.
3. By the hour (varying rates, depending upon skills and equipment required, etc.).
4. Program development.
5. Various consulting capabilities.
6. Certain specialized tasks (banking services, payroll, seismic processing) based on unit transaction costs.
7. Unit charges for CPU cycles.

Time-sharing Terminals

Time-sharing is a procedure allowing many persons to use the same computer. This process has been highly refined in the past few years. The number and types of benefits offered to the user have increased very dramatically. Proliferation of equipment and computing power has made use of a time-sharing terminal almost common usage in many facets of everyday life. There are terminals available on college campuses, bringing computing power to the lowest undergraduate. Likewise, there are devices available to children in elementary schools. Time-sharing devices have the advantage of bringing computing power and logic into the hands of the end user. At the same time, there develops an interaction between person and computer where entering of data directly into the computer is a quick, easy means of conversing directly with the machine.

The substitution of electronic speeds can do much to satisfy, or stimulate, the inquiring mind of a young student. It cannot be a substitute for the teacher, but it can encourage a young brain to develop more rapidly. Likewise for the architectural engineer who is faced with the task of calculating stress factors for a highrise office building, computing power, through a time-sharing terminal, eliminates or reduces the need for slide-rule calculations and interpretations. A terminal also has the capacity to call out standard formulas on a moment's notice, thus freeing an architect for productive effort and reducing the "housekeeping" required for writing numbers on paper and transcribing results. Time-sharing operations are priced differently from conventional service bureaus. This can result in increased user satisfaction and benefits.

Some operations will, like the conventional service operation, offer a bewildering number of resources with a seemingly complicated pricing schedule. The options that may be available are:

1. Free use of all resident packages (no charge made for using standard, predeveloped software routines).
2. Your choice of terminals (CRT's with or without printing, terminals with printer output, etc.) at your cost and selection.
3. Telephone line costs may be a chargeable item.
4. Slight additional charges for other computer resources (printers, tape drives, disk drives).
5. Ongoing charges (referred to as "connect" time).
6. Additional costs of forms, cards, postage, mailing expenses and other incidentals.

If the end-user examines each individual line-item charge, the apparent cost will appear reasonable. As the data processing overseer, your concern must be with total cumulative effect of these charges. The unrestricted, unmonitored usage of a terminal *can* lead to horrendous costs that bring little benefit to the project at hand. You could discard the time-sharing concept as too expensive based solely on costs. If the time-sharing concept was not acceptable, the procedure would have perished in the marketplace. One function of the data processing manager is to provide desirable alternatives. A time-sharing terminal provides an attractive alternative when carefully controlled and monitored.

Remote Job Entry

Remote job entry (RJE) is the submission of an entire job through a remote terminal into a central computer complex. After processing (which may include several procedures and programs), the finished product may then be returned to the person or department through the same RJE terminal. In its original state RJE was a relatively simple device. With the availability of increased power at individual office or substation levels, RJE terminals have become increasingly sophisticated—with core storage and varying degrees of programmable capabilities. As technology becomes more diffused through the organization, an RJE terminal can be enhanced with more powerful options. The net result of this technology infusion is to bring total computing capabilities close to the ultimate user. In instances such as a nationwide distribution operation, the RJE may be represented in the form of an IBM System 3 to forward a finished product (edited, balanced, and audited for accuracy) to a large computer complex thousands of miles away. As a service administrator, you may have the opportunity to participate in decisions involving these devices, whether they be a "dumb" IBM 3741 Model 1, or a complete system for forwarding data to corporate headquarters. The power is available. Your task is to consider the potential costs and benefits before accepting or rejecting remote job entry.

Resource Decisions

There is no simple, easy rule to follow in making decisions for utilizing the options of computing power. Small engineering offices may need only an electronic desk calculator; others may require a terminal for each engineer on the payroll. Other operations may need centralized computing power and "call-up" capabilities at distant job sites. A manufacturing enterprise may need sales information from branch installations to plan for allocation of production capabilities. A selling organization may have a need for monitoring sales on a rapid, up-to-date basis.

A decision for decentralization of computing power (not the actual installation) is not one to be made lightly. In every situation, basic factors of available personnel, hardware, and money must be carefully appraised. Resulting decisions should have the net effect of achieving company goals and strengthening your role. In suggesting these options, time is introduced as a factor.

With only twenty-four hours in a day, time is a critical resource.

To attain a competitive position in the marketplace, reaction time between decision and action must be reduced. There are many examples in history where the time element was absolutely crucial to the success or failure of an enterprise. IBM, with a heavy commitment of resources, made the 1401 series into an almost instant success. This "instant success" as much as anything else, was based on timing and decisions. In addition, the market was at the right point in time. One other example: In the movie *Patton*, every general was faced with crucial decisions, many of them based on time weighted by other factors. There are many elements of time in your shop. Schedules must be met. Reports must be prepared and distributed in time for the sales or director's meeting. Decisions must be made, based on money.

The cost and benefits of outside services are factors that can be readily measured. Measure these costs and benefits carefully. Their usage may spell the difference between profit and loss. Time, as an asset not utilized, is lost and can never be regained or recouped. The outside service provides a manager with additional capabilities that may be necessary in acting as a professional data processing manager. A computer cycle is measured in milliseconds, inexorably ticking away resources of your operation. It is your duty to utilize these milliseconds—in any machine.

Review Questions

1.   Be prepared to discuss in detail, pro and con, how outside computing services would affect your position as DP manager (in a manufacturing environment).

2.   Your employer is allowing other departments to negotiate individual contracts for computer services. Are there circumstances in which this would be desirable? If so, describe.

3.   Using a Model 15 and a 1403 N-1 is sufficient for most of the processing and print needs for normal requirements. Monthly requirements dictate a need for an additional 100 hours of print time. What are your recommendations to management for handling this overload? Timing is a problem.

4.   Your employer, a wholesale distributor serving the needs of three states through multiple distribution centers and 32 salespersons, has successfully installed a Model 12 to handle the processing load. After meeting all requirements and recommendations from the original proposal, the equipment is operating at approximately 60% of capacity. Assuming usual applications for sales analysis, inventory control, billing, and accounts receivable, what are your recommendations for the next application? You may consider general ledger, accounts payable, payroll, or any other profitable application.

chapter 3

Selection
of Services

Guidelines and checkpoints can be used in selection of a product or service. Points to be considered for choosing or evaluating the exact form of outside computer services are not readily and quickly defined. You should be prepared to formulate a specialized checklist of prerequisites. This will enable fashioning a set of standards designed to fill unique needs within your organization. For example, a service bureau specializing in hospitals and medical clinics might lack those qualities needed for a firm of consulting engineers. Other firms in your industry may have varying needs due to differing degrees of emphasis placed on management functions. Use your list of standards rather than blindly following industry practices.

When the search begins—assuming the need has been justified through research—there are certain items that should be scrutinized for all outside commercial services. A partial list of some checkpoints and comments includes:

Financial. Is the operation stable? Does it have adequate financial resources to handle your project? Are there indications of impending fiscal troubles? Will the company provide you with a statement of financial condition? What sort of arrangements for payment will be expected? Can you check through the services of Dun and Bradstreet? An agency is not obligated to furnish all of the above, but you should beware of the organization that is very evasive about providing some requested information. One other measure of financial stability—how long have they been in operation?

Technical Qualifications. What kind, and how many years of experience are available from the staff? Do they understand your particular application, or do they promise everything? Can you visit with the systems or programmer types who will be working with you? Too much emphasis has been made concerning "personality conflicts," but if you cannot have a good working relationship with the personnel assigned to your account, you may have a severe problem.

Ferreting out the difference between proficiency in an application and mere familiarity should be a part of your checklist.

Hardware. Does the service operate its hardware, or does it lease time from another user? If so, the charges for their services could reflect some lower differential. Is the hardware suitable for your needs—not too much power and certainly not too little? Is the configuration, including peripherals, adequate? What are the security arrangements for emergency backup? Is their hardware compatible with your own equipment? Regardless of the exact hardware requirements, your application should be relatively portable between at least two or more similar systems. This suggests certain standards and requirements which relate back to the question—can they do the job that I am expecting?

Software. This can be the most crucial question involved in selection of an outside service vendor. Does the software exist? If so, who owns it, and what are your rights in the processing of data? If the software is to be written, who will own the package—source code, documentation, and object code? Will the software be portable between systems, and configurations? If the firm goes out of business, what happens to your software? If new programs are proprietary to your firm, what provisions will be made for insuring exclusivity? In the event of software failure, who is responsible? Who will bear costs of repairing the damage? If the software is to be new and unique for your organization, it is your absolute responsibility to have totally defined all parameters and requirements. In case of software failure, it is your responsibility and duty to examine the reasons and affix responsibility. It may be your problem due to an ill-defined task. It may be a mutual responsibility for both parties. Software can be analogous to a legal contract. Without bilateral understanding, a valid contract cannot exist. If your purchased software does not meet specifications, then the task is not finished. By opting for software from an outside service, your decision has been made to buy—not build. It may be more convenient for the short term to buy, but in so doing, you are abdicating some degree of responsibility and losing a certain amount of project control.

Contracts. No longer is a man's word as good as his bond. Most existing contracts for computer equipment, hardware or software, have various disclaimers. These disclaimers frequently are in boldface type, denying responsibility for any provisions not included and made a part of the original contract. Witness the following example:

The Customer acknowledges that he has read this Agreement, including all printed language, understands it and agrees to be bound by its terms and further, agrees that it is the complete and exclusive statement of the agreement between the parties, which supersedes all proposals oral or written and all other communications between the parties relating to the subject matter of this Agreement.

The example clearly spells out the legal responsibities for *both* parties. If you deem a contract unnecessary, the least amount of protection that you can buy is a letter of intent, or understanding. It may be undesirable or uneconomical to have a contract for certain services, but a minimum letter would carefully define, for your mutual satisfaction, prices and performance. Any oral, or verbal, promises must be included and made a part of the agreement. In case of a misunderstanding as to actual definition for contract compliance, a formal contract will be the ultimate authority. If the misunderstandings still exist after lengthy, informal negotiations, litigation may be the only answer—expensive though it may be.

Summarizing Your Options

Caveat emptor. "Let the buyer beware." The overworked Latin phrase is still a truism. As in other phases of supervision, planning is of the essence. Planning time spent in advance of actual project production is more than repaid in user satisfaction with the successful completion of a contract mutually satisfactory to all parties. The factors are there—types of services, hardware, software, etc., and other items to be considered. If it is your responsibility to make the final choice of available options, then it is also your duty to your employer to minimize and reduce the exposure to danger. It is your obligation to insure that purchased services are compatible with your needs.

Review Questions

1.   On the assumption your employer is allowing certain departments to use outside services for computing needs, how would you define your position on this matter? If the contracts are negotiated without your participation, do you have any continuing responsibility?

2.   Beyond conventional applications covered in the original pro-

posal, whose responsibility is it to add new applications as continuing and additional justification for the equipment?

3.   A contract is usually written and supplied by the vendor. What are the benefits accruing to the user from acceptance of this standard contract? What is the effect of this contract upon any verbal promises made by the sales representative?

chapter 4

Your Role
as a Manager

The planning function is, according to Koontz and O'Donnell in their book, *Principles of Management*: ". . . one of the functions of the manager and as such involves the selection from among alternatives of enterprise objectives, policies, procedures, and programs. It is thus decision-making affecting the entire course of an enterprise."[1]

The Role of the Departmental Manager

Your position as the DP manager must remain true and constant to this basic management principle of planning. Methods remain the same. Resources may bear dissimilar names, and responsibilities may be different in degree, but planning is a basic role. With weak or insubstantial planning, the role of the DP shop will suffer. Planning is the basis for future decisions. Other functions of a manager are to be included and made part of the planning process. There are many theories of management and management structure, each with varying emphasis. With due respect to all theories, your basic duties as a DP manager are:

1. Planning.
2. Organizing.
3. Controlling.
4. Staffing.
5. Directing.

[1] Harold Koontz and Cyril O'Donnell, *Principles of Management* (New York: McGraw-Hill Book Company, 1955), p. 429.

This skeletal outline of functions tends to ignore the actual tasks of motivation and leadership. Basic requirements will be dictated for the job even before the position is filled. Undefinable skills of motivation and leadership must be among those attributes you bring to your position as an overseer of DP. To understand these supervisory tasks as they relate to DP, we must consider each as a separate entity.

The Planning Function

"Quite simply, planning involves recycling and rethinking what is needed tomorrow and not just repeating yesterday's successes."[2] Although this is a general truth, it has special relevance to the computer. From this concept, we may proceed to consider planning duties in three forms:

1. Immediate.
2. Short-range.
3. Long-term.

For our purposes, we shall consider an immediate need as a need to be satisfied within a time period less than *one month*. Short-range plans may be less than a month, but more frequently will involve a cycle of more than one but perhaps less than six months. Long-term planning will be more than an absolute minimum of six months and possibly extending for four to five years in the process of constant re-evaluation to meet proposed requirements based on some future situation. Without an infallible crystal ball, the planning cycle must of necessity be changed, shifted, and rearranged in responding to a changing environment. Planning cannot be perfect *or* infallible. Planning is, and should be, a methodical procedure designed to provide an acceptable course of action for increasing profit opportunities and minimizing exposure to costly alternative risks.

Immediate planning phases may be brief and cursory in nature. It may consist of a head count of the staff or a simple forms inventory required for the coming week. Vacation schedules must be examined and provisions made for additional help, as necessary. Certain requests for immediate action may be phased into the normal schedule. Immediate planning may be more accurate due to the short interval of time between

---

[2] Kit Grindley and John Humble, *The Effective Computer*, AMACOM, a Division of American Management Association (McGraw-Hill Publishing Company (UK) Limited), p. 141.

proposal and implementation. Prospects for planning success in the immediate phase are very good. The time lapse is much shorter, and future happenings may be predicted with a higher degree of success.

The longer the time span, the greater chance there is for error in the planning cycle. Immediate planning may be related to the law of physics: For every action, there is an opposite and equal reaction. Hurried decisions may cause even more "snap" future decisions. This does not imply the immediate aspects of the cycle should bear the stigma of quick, off-the-cuff decisions. Planning must always consider future prospects for success or failure.

Decision-making for the immediate term may have long-range implications that will impact subsequent planning steps for the future. As a manager, you should be aware of the possible effect of immediate decisions as they relate to long-term and short-range strategy. For example, a long-term decision involving print size and line spacing may affect your organization for many years. Be wary of the quick and easy decisions as you may have to live with them for an extended period.

It is ever so tempting for a manager to make expedient decisions. The future may see adoption of these decisions as if they were written on tablets of stone to become doctrine for the entire company. Perhaps this is not all bad, but careful consideration of all decisions will facilitate implementation of planning for the longer term.

The characteristics of short-range planning offer the most potential for great success over the total cycle from inception to implementation. The past is gone—but not forgotten—thus encouraging you to learn and profit from past successes *and failures*. The future is supposedly at a distant point ahead in time, and the potential for careful organizing can be recognized. The constraints of time are present without immediate demands for quick benefits. In this phase of the cycle, there is not the quick rush for sudden action and hasty decisions. You may devote personal time and attention, or that of your staff, to consideration of troublesome checkpoints arising in the concept phase. It is indeed rare for you, or any manager, to foresee in their entirety, all potential problems that may arise.

Careful attention to detail, with well thought-out decisions, will have the benefit of reducing unforeseen surprises and increasing the benefits derived from careful deliberation. Generally, hurried decisions are undesirable. If projections are reasonably adequate, including allowances for these unforeseen happenings, the pressure for immediate decisions will be lessened. It would appear that you need a tight forecast with provisions for a quick (loose) response. This is not the case. Your design must be tight, including allowances for reasonable, and unpredictable occurrences that may arise. Anticipation of the future may be worse than reality, but the chances for harmful damage are greatly reduced by a careful fabrication of plans.

Long-range projection is one of the most neglected areas of management responsibility. You may tend to ignore it due to your management's inability to furnish a blueprint for the future. Long-range projects cannot foresee all allowances for the introduction of new processes into factory or computer installations. With these hindrances, the opportunity to withdraw from long-range strategies is very great. These are only excuses providing unreasonable justification for not taking time to anticipate the future. In my own installation, for example, our short-range plans included decentralization of data entry functions with implementation of IBM 3741 and 3742 devices. Long-range plans included implementation of CRT's; immediate plans were to use the 3741 as a transitional device. Short-range plans called for de-centralization of data entry, though this evolved over a period of months and years. The most important lesson to be learned in this example is the fortuitous combination of all cycle phases and timing.

Circumstances afforded management the opportunity to move carefully (immediate) into a new process (short-range) without a total commitment (long-term) of corporate resources to a single plan of action. The opportunity to plan and react as situations changed gave strength and flexibility to the program. With careful integration of the three cycles of planning, you may be able to achieve the same successes. Careful application of logic in the design portion has the desired effect of minimizing surprises and deriving increased benefits from another resource—time. In your daily cycle, there should be measurable time devoted to projecting future needs. The old aphorism holds true: Plan your work and work your plan. Some definable amount of time in your daily schedule *must* be devoted to blocking out a design for the future.

A beehive, or a child's ant farm, is representative of a complete, self-contained organization. It may be said that organization is the function of bringing order into an unordered situation. The organization of the insect farm is highly structured, devoted to preservation of the whole. A business organization may have a greater degree of interest diversification, but the organization nurtures the unit and increases relative power of the organization. In this context, the organization of a business enterprise is a fluid structure adapting to changing needs in the marketplace. The basic framework may remain much the same but will undergo sweeping revisions in reaction to external forces. Therefore, we may recognize the concept of organization as an outline within certain boundaries and perimeters.

Organization of the DP function will be similar to that of the overall organization. There will be delegated responsibilities, and certain authorities, for purposes of internal control. Even so, the machine installation will be subject to additional internal needs and external forces. This shifting of organizational resources may be considered a combination of action, reaction, and an interaction of changing relationships.

The defined organization of the DP function may be very simple as shown in Figure 1, or it may be as complex as the example shown in Figure 2 on the next page. In both instances, we see a major grouping of these tasks:

1. Management.
2. Programming and systems.
3. Operations.
4. Data entry.

This list is not inclusive and indicates only major headings. From the charts, you can see defined lines of responsibility for these assigned duties. There are implied lines of authority and responsibility. As the organization grows in complexity, additional duties will be added to the basics to allow for inclusion of new specialized skills. This does not imply a functional change but rather the reaction of an organism to meet increasing needs.

Within your organization, you should create specific lines of authority and responsibility. The amount of formality is related to size of the enterprise but will follow basic functional lines. As in the corporate table of organization, your internal chart should have carefully drawn lines of command and accountability. Delineation of duties serves to fix responsibility for named functional areas. These assignments carry implications of sufficient power to resolve internal mission assignments. Many advantages are derived from this formalized structure. In a changing environment, you always have the opportunity to confer with your internal department heads. If selected duties have been assigned, there will be no need (in the beginning) to have a joint meeting for discussing all aspects of change. You will have the opportunity to discuss possibilities of change, and its effect, with the programming manager, the data entry supervisor, and your operations manager. The benefit derived from individual consultation far exceeds loss of productive time. Later, a joint meeting will be required to discuss and announce decisions affecting the entire department. Efficient grouping of duties will also follow natural lines of control.

Internal Departmental Structure

Internal structure of your department should be simple. There are management principles as to the maximum number of people who can be effectively supervised by one person, but the one rule that is easiest to follow and implement is to keep it simple. As size increases, there will be

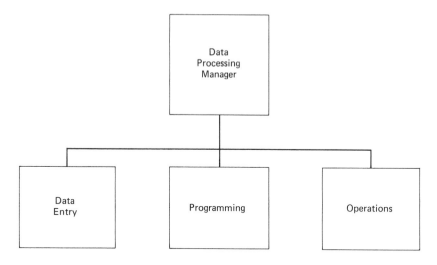

Figure 1

higher degrees of skill specialization. Organizations may be rearranged to accommodate specialties, but the principle of simplicity should be observed.

A logical structure provides the framework to allow for orderly growth. The framework creates an atmosphere of internal discipline needed in establishing formal lines of jurisdiction and accountability.

Controlling

The control function follows that of planning. Without planning, there cannot exist reasonable control. According to *The Management of Organizations* by Hicks and Gullett, "Controlling is the process by which management sees if what did happen was supposed to happen. If not, necessary adjustments are made . . . ."[3]

In establishing the control function for your department, it becomes necessary to create standards of performance. External controls may be naturally built into your procedures as a logical extension and outgrowth of acceptable accounting and shop management policies. In the application of accounting controls, perhaps most prevalent is the use of predetermined controls and totals, i.e., if it does not balance at this point, don't go any further; or a control document count indicates 492 transactions, and the computer printout reflects 486. Rules may be estab-

---

[3] Herbert G. Hicks and C. Ray Gullett, *The Management of Organizations*, 3rd ed. (New York: McGraw-Hill Book Company).

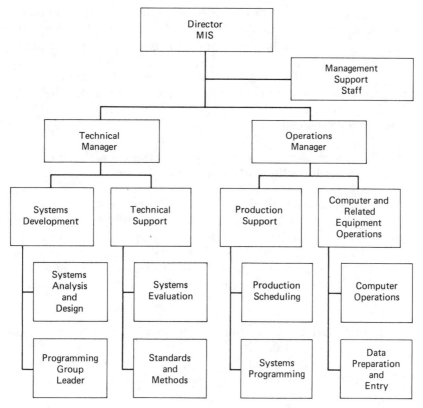

Figure 2

lished by departments outside your jurisdiction and are easily enforceable. Controls should be established to measure and monitor progress toward achieving goals originally defined in planning. The power of the computer, coupled with effective controls, provides a superior combination of management tools.

Controlling is not limited to the implementation of certain mechanical checkpoints. Control is a process used to insure effective performance. A receiving clerk checking quantities of raw material is performing a control function. The sales manager comparing actual sales with projections is deeply involved with control. The security guard checking badges and I.D.'s is performing a vital function. In your department, it is your responsibility to assist in establishing and maintaining corporate controls. It is solely your responsibility to establish internal regulations for your installation. This would include internal checkpoints and standards for programming, data entry, systems, etc.

Internal control procedures for data processing may cross departmental lines. There are basic approaches that have proven effective in many installations. Some of these techniques, or methods, are described briefly. These processes have been successful in other situations. These proposals, if accepted, should be adapted to your specific requirements.

Time Stamp. Use of a time stamp for work flow (*in* and *out*) provides a means of judging effectiveness of scheduling. It also provides a record of performance for external departments charged with responsibilities for meeting your production schedules.

Document Control. A simple journal or log of all documents for processing is easy to institute and documents the flow of work units.

Daily Machine Production Log and Schedule. The act of preparing a production log is effective in providing you with records of machine utilization and production times. A schedule, prepared in advance, is also very effective when used and enforced. It may be used in conjunction with all other documents, or more properly, it will serve as a planning guide for known variations from a normal schedule (month-end or quarterly reports).

Documentation. The topic of documentation will be discussed later but is so important that it must be mentioned under control procedures. Most programming languages and compilers allow for programmer-supplied comments and documentation. These should be used freely and frequently.

Central Storage of Programs and Records. This is a basic point, but frequently overlooked. Unless certain basic procedures and policies are instituted, you could lose control of all programs and files.

Policy Manual. This sometimes overlooked procedure can answer many questions and help reinforce policy procedures for the department.

Many of these points will be discussed separately in other chapters, and this list is not complete. Certain detailed operating procedures may require specific controls outside the province of these mentioned items. If desirable and necessary, install the controls. Controls are designed to enforce certain standards of performance at all company levels; however, without reasonable restraint, it is possible to over-control. Controls, to be effective, must be simple and meaningful. If cumbersome manual procedures are implemented for control purposes, the system will almost surely fail. The establishment of controls provides a simple scheme to measure and report on planning effectiveness.

Directing

Directing, in one sense of the word, may be the issuing of commands or directives. In another broader sense of the word, you may view directing as a function lending purpose to the organization. Without a defined "sense of direction," an organization may flounder aimlessly. In terms of internal departmental supervision, we will be examining the direction function using both definitions. A director of a motion picture or television drama embodies this duality of functions. His attitudes and feelings about an upcoming drama will impart a sense of direction to the enterprise. Issued orders and directives represent a more active application of the directing task.

In establishing a sense of direction for an installation, you are in fact manufacturing a broad framework of policy. It is comparable to accepting a task or program assignment. The mission might be to automate those functions that lend themselves to computer discipline, or it may be more narrowly defined as specific elimination of costly delays in paperwork processing. How you regard this assignment will result in an ultimate sense of direction for the department. Your personal attitude will guide and set the tone for future applications. If you tend to regard a task as onerous, then you may expect this same attitude to be reflected in your staff. A general positive air of confidence and the welcoming of challenges may do much to lend not only a sense of direction, but will go far in establishing a sense of purpose for your installation.

The issuing of an order, command, or directive is a necessary part of directing. How you perceive your role as a supervisor of an installation will influence your attitude as an order-giver. The art of managing has not been so well-defined as to furnish you with infallible techniques and methods applicable in a particular situation. The careful application of your own style and method of management techniques can produce effective results. There are times when you ask your staff to work with you. In other instances, you must behave in an autocratic fashion, issuing clear, concise orders leaving little to the imagination. For some situations, you may need to set an example and goal for others to achieve. Your directions, and how they are accepted, will determine the success of your managerial efforts. As a member of management, you are charged with the responsibility for getting things done through the efforts of your staff and the capabilities of the equipment.

In the issuance of instructions and assignments to your staff, you will be imparting a sense of direction needed to accomplish these tasks. Your skills in conveying to your staff a sense of commitment will set the tone for the shop. Do not let this opportunity pass by. The spirit of the office is established by you, the manager. If you contribute a sense of urgency to the entire operation, you have in effect established a goal, or standard of performance. Establishment of standards will decrease the time required for directing the staff. Standards are an adjunct to your efforts in supplying the sense of direction.

Staffing

In its purest form, staffing may be the hiring of personnel to perform certain defined job tasks. Needs of a corporation may dictate detailed, comprehensive personnel requirements, differing only in detail and additional considerations existing in the organization. The building of a staff is more complex than simply supplying personnel to fill various job openings. Staffing for an installation is a supervisory responsibility and cannot be totally delegated to the personnel department. Competent personnel are the key to future success in meeting job requirements.

Creating a working team is much more than a simple matching or pairing of personnel and job descriptions. Staffing is rather a careful matching, or blending, of available skills and talents to meet present and future needs. It is unlikely that the nature of any job will remain unchanged over the years. Likewise, employees are not remaining static. As the company grows, personnel should be encouraged to develop. Careful attention to staffing needs provides a nucleus and framework for internal growth in developing staff potential.

In staffing the small DP installation, you should give separate but equal attention to requirements for each available position. A small shop is apt to be informal and relatively close-knit. This environment requires the staffing function to meet stated job requirements without seriously disturbing the existing structure. Informal groups may exert influence on hiring, but the needs of a corporation cannot be subordinated to interoffice structures.

Staffing requirements are effectively met in combination with "promote-from within" policy. The filling of future job openings from within may serve to increase entry level standards. With increased standards and requirements, the level of the position may be raised. Promoting from within offers the employee visual recognition and reward for on-the-job performance. This is not to imply that all employees are considered candidates for top management. It does suggest that potential employees must be "trainable and promotable."

Some disadvantages and restraints may occur from always promoting from within. For example, a new job position may be created requiring new skills not available internally. If this is the case, a job assignment may require instant proficiency, and outside hiring is dictated.

There are implications of position status in formal job titles when staffing an organization. Expedient decisions for the new job may create additional staffing problems. Future estimates may dictate present prerequisites in building a strong, cohesive group.

Summarizing

Basic management functions have been named and discussed to a limited degree in this chapter. There can be no reasonable way of measuring relative importance of each function in your job. Only you can be aware of total value placed on the job assignments by management. The press of work may be used as an excuse for inadequate planning, but there is no reason for complete absence of future preparation. One suggestion for creating a future strategy: Set a definite time in your schedule (before, during, or after work) to be devoted to the planning function. This time may be limited or restricted, but planning must be accomplished. In the smaller shop you may plan during a long production run when the equipment requires little operator intervention. How or when the planning is performed is of no significance. Planning may be accomplished anytime—formally or informally—but must be done. A poor, ineffective proposal is better than no strategy at all. "For want of a nail, the shoe was lost . . . ."

Review Questions

1.   The five major activities and duties of a manager are concerned with planning, organizing, controlling, directing and staffing. Which is more important than the others? Explain why.

2.   Define the differences between immediate, short-range, and long-term planning.

3.   In examining an organizational chart, you may find that data entry is given separate but equal status along with programming and operations. Is this a valid concept?

4.   In planning for future applications, how would you integrate a system into one homogeneous entity?

5.   Promoting from within is a worthy policy, though there are certain limitations. Name four advantages and disadvantages.

6.   There are certain techniques to be effectively used in establishing control over an installation. Describe how you would utilize the following methods:

(a) Document control

(b) Time stamping

(c) Production logs and schedules

(d) Policy manuals

chapter 5

After
the Decision

Your company has reached the decision to have computer power in-house. It may be a small System 32, it may be an expanded Model 12, a full-blown Model 15, or perhaps an IBM 370/115 or 125. In most cases, the final determination was made on a basis of "only this many dollars for so much computing power." This glib phrase carries with it the implication, if it doesn't work out, well, we can always send it back because we have so little invested in it. This may be true, but it is only a small piece of the iceberg. Corporate dollars invested in an installation are far more than the quoted monthly lease price. Your compensation package helps to raise the price of automation. The relatively small amount of required floor space is not furnished by the equipment vendor; nor is electric power, air conditioning, and any special wiring. When the "total" package is put together, combined amounts will greatly exceed quoted monthly lease prices for the equipment. The cost of forms and supplies, though involving a certain amount of cost substitution, will increase with machine utilization.

Your task as supervisor of an installation is to monitor closely all costs and provide management with the best services available at the lowest price. Alternative leasing options may be listed under four major categories:

1. 30-day open-end lease.
2. Purchase.
3. Third-party leasing.
4. Term leases with option to buy.

Each of the four major available options offers certain advantages and limitations.

The final decision will probably be made at a management level above the DP manager. Your recommendations should be based on best estimates for suitability of a configuration in the foreseeable future. Requirements of an organization are subject to many external conditions in the marketplace, and it is dereliction of duty to assume today's purchase will meet and fulfill all predictable needs for the next five years. A corporation will not remain static, and the same is true of equipment. The configuration necessary to process today's work volumes may be totally inadequate to meet needs one to two years in the future.

From prior experience, I have learned that a tendency of management is to regard all office hardware as a necessary evil that will absorb all new projects easily and never wear out or become obsolete.

This attitude makes a decision for leasing or buying of equipment more critical. In addition, technological advancements being announced almost daily may render your equipment obsolete long before the end of its useful life. You must carefully consider each option in its entirety before recommending a decision. This judgment is not a final act. It is a reasonable, well thought-out action designed to meet a particular need over a reasonable amount of time.

The 30-Day Open-end Lease

Few vendors are willing to gamble on equipment proving its worth during the first 30 days. Indeed, IBM with its available resources will not gamble on a 30-day trial period, in a contract. Other vendors who are less affluent are even more reluctant to gamble on the outcome of a timed wager with circumstances beyond their control. Many vendors are willing to warrant certain pieces of equipment earning their keep inside a reasonable time frame, but it is not easy to discard an entire installation at a moment's notice.

The purest 30-day notice is exactly what the name implies. At the end of 30 day's written notice, equipment may be returned to the lessor without financial penalty. This does not mean the vendor is being altruistic. Quite the reverse is true: A written letter of cancellation places the vendor on notice that a customer has excess equipment, or a potential problem may be developing. The 90-day cancellation serves the same purpose, except the vendor has a longer time frame to marshal resources and "re-sell" the account, if need be. This short-term cancellation clause also gives you the option of ordering equipment to meet a peak load situation without extreme financial penalties.

In basic contracts involving IBM hardware, you have the option of cancelling a portion of the leased equipment (on written 30-day notice) as long as the CPU and/or total rent does not go below a certain specified minimum. The same holds true for other contracts, but restrictions are spelled out in much detail, giving the user a lesser degree of flexibility.

If cost considerations are of paramount importance, the 30-day open-end lease is probably the most expensive option available. Prices are high; money flows one-way; and at expiration of the cancelled contract, a user has a blank space in the machine room and cancelled checks available for papering the walls. This short-term option offers services at a price—value received for value paid. Some circumstances are such that a 30-day contract is the best available financial choice. For example, a department store may need additional data entry capacity to handle holiday season peak loads. The rest of the year, this equipment might gather dust. Using this 30-day option, the manager can respond to a necessary situation without impacting long-range considerations for personnel or equipment. Under cases such as the one described above, the 30-day lease with options becomes an attractive alternative.

The 30-day short-term contract has its place in your shop. Like accessories on an automobile, there are desirable features that carry a cost and inherent value. Your job is to measure expenses—and benefits. Once benefits have been measured, a decision becomes a matter of value judgment.

The Extended Term Plan Option

This user option has the benefit of reducing monthly outlays for rental equipment over a defined period of time. The cost of the option is in the user's agreement to keep the equipment for a certain amount of time—carefully defined in the contract. This particular contract may be of value when the user is relatively certain of short-term needs and there are no indications or prospects for impending mergers or reorganization. ETP contracts usually contain buy-out provisions, ranging from relatively cheap to fairly expensive; dependent upon hardware and terms of the agreement. This method includes the desirable factor of accruing purchase options and provides a limited degree of hedging against purchased equipment being made obsolete by new technology.

When an organization is in a rapid state of change, it may not be desirable to exercise the ETP option. This would be apparent if you were considering a printer upgrade from an IBM 5203 at 300 lines per minute (lpm) to a 1403 with a print speed of 465 lpm. The first jump to 465 lpm offers a 50% increase in print speeds. The next step is to 600 lpm and is followed by the 1403 N-1 with a rated capacity of 1100 lpm. (In this example, we have referred to the IBM 1403 series; but there are other fine printers available.) Organizational print needs vary widely by time of the month and predictable numbers of new applications to be considered for the future. In situations similar to the one described above, it may be in your best interest, as a thinking manager, to avoid ETP provisions until demand is sufficiently stable to warrant higher speeds—and an extended term. Financial benefits of ETP may appear to be long-term; but benefits accruing to your installation over an ETP term by *not* using the option may be greater. Of course, buy-out provisions should be made a part of the financial consideration. This will allow you the opportunity of making a decision involving only slight financial impact, and yet reducing present monthly costs.

In emphasizing printer options, do not overlook other leased items. Be sure to pay the same amount of careful attention to contract provisions available for all peripheral units. In doing this, be aware that each unit, or family of units, may have varying discounts under ETP provisions, and purchase accruals may have different percentages.

Where possible, it may be even more desirable to place selected units on a staggered leasing term arrangement, rather than placing all data entry gear in a contract with common beginning and expiration dates; arrange the agreement(s) so the contracts for each unit (or units) go into effect, and expire, over an extended number of months. This allows you the option of renewing on a staggered due date, options for letting the term totally expire, and more important, the careful phasing in of new equipment on a planned basis.

ETP is your asset. Used carefully and wisely, it could prevent the costly embarrassment of financial penalties and/or technological obsolescence, and reduce current expenses.

Fixed Term Plan

The fixed term plan offered by IBM is not available on every piece of hardware nor is it suitable for every situation. One of the prime advantages offered by FTP is a fixed guarantee of price. This form of price protection gives the user a fixed price for a number of years and does not restrict equipment to single-shift usage. The most singular drawback is its inflexibility. Penalties for early buy-out are very restrictive and almost prohibitive. If your organization is in a period of rapid expansion brought about by growth, mergers, or acquisitions, this option can lock you into a particular CPU (and configuration by implication) that could severely restrict future response to a new environment. Companies in relatively stable situations would do well to investigate and evaluate financial benefits to be derived from FTP.

At the risk of repetition, this option is an asset. Its potential must be evaluated carefully before rejection, or acceptance.

Outright Purchase

Outright purchase offers excellent potential for a reduction of direct costs. Financial rewards may also be significant. As with other plans, many factors overlap with varying amounts of emphasis. Obsolescence, corporate growth, and configurations are major considerations to be very carefully weighed.[4]

As with FTP, purchase has the tendency to "lock in" a particular CPU and configuration. The key to purchase, while retaining flexibility, is to project equipment needs for the future. If, after due weighing of the factors involved, a purchase is indicated, then you should consider additional possibilities for future hardware expansion. Does your configuration come in at the bottom of the line, or are you buying near the upper limits of expansion capabilities? To buy at the upper limits is to self-impose restrictions on machine growth. A minimum configuration, at the bottom of the line, may allow for internal expansion without significant CPU changes. A decision to purchase will involve a significant expenditure of capital funds. In a management presentation you would do well to describe all options early on in the presentation, presenting an orderly plan for future needs based on a reasonable projection of costs, needs, and benefits. This presentation should also point out the pitfalls of purchasing, including obsolescence. If, once the decision has been made, you must go back to the investment committee for a newer, more expensive model, you may lose credibility.

Obsolescence is something of a specter. Threat of a technological breakthrough is always lurking in the future. However, in recent years we

---

[4] My present employer entered data processing in 1964 with a limited configuration of unit-record equipment. By 1976, the company had grown and evolved through an IBM 360/20 card system, a System 3/10 disk system, a System 3/model 15, tape and disk, into a 370/125-2 with disk and tape. In retrospect, financial opportunities were missed in failure to purchase the Model 10 and the Model 15. The various factors were considered and rejected. The 370 is a purchased machine.

have seen comparatively small technological advancements instead of a major step through an unknown barrier. It appears that new innovations will be evolutionary in character, thus discounting the threat of overnight obsolescence. A new process may nullify future plans for DP growth, but it will not negate a purchase decision made on the basis of current facts available at hand; and even if it did, such a displacement would occur only after careful consideration of alternatives.

Factory equipment tends to have a well-defined life cycle, i.e., it will produce x amount of product over a fairly predictable life span. This relationship does not hold true in quite such rigid terms for EDP equipment. The rate of failure for certain electronic components may be rated as 20,000 hours MTBF (mean time between failures), and this is only a statistical projection for one component. With proper maintenance, a computer may be expected to last well over a decade, and some parts may never wear out. This fact will tend to extend the effective life of your computer and reduce threats of obsolescence.

It then behooves the purchaser to make maximum use of this asset. Many small- to medium-sized shops tend to regard a DP operation as a machine to be operated on a 40-hour basis. This is not the case. A computer is designed to run and run and run. Cost per hour, when utilized for more than one shift, makes the purchase option even more attractive.

Maintenance contracts do not truthfully reflect charges for maintenance. Costed effectively, a maintenance contract should be considered as insurance. That is, the manufacturer is assuming cost of any possible replacement parts and labor regardless of equipment failure. I/O gear, subject to higher mechanical wear and deterioration, may bear greater maintenance charges. It should be fairly obvious that purchase costs when amortized over an indefinite number of productive hours, may reflect a wise financial decision. Any new factor does not change the basis of the original financial consideration. The original purchase decision cannot be changed by hindsight or retrospection.

Third-party Leasing

Soon after the Supreme Court directed IBM (in 1956) to make equipment available for purchase, equipment leasing companies filled the yellow pages of many metropolitan telephone directories. The financial experts were quick to recognize potential benefits of leasing an electronic computer. The agreements were extremely solid, and when the lease expired, the equipment was still in marketable condition. This allows a profit for the lessee, benefits of a guaranteed lease for the user, and the lessor inherits problems of used equipment ownership at the end of a lease term.

Subject to financial changes and new hardware developments, the third-party leasing arrangement offers advantages over outright purchase of equipment. The advantages are there particularly when a company is allowed to take advantage of a lease involving no firm commitments of capital. A lease is an expense item with no depreciation charges to compute; whereas a purchase involves a commitment of cash early in the process.

Is a third-party lease good for your situation? The only answer is a strong maybe—with reservations. The cost of money (yours or theirs) is always a factor. A leasing company may, or may not, have favorable financing arrangements with a financial institution. Your own firm may negotiate the same arrangements. By opting for the third party, your company avoids the necessity of making a firm purchase agreement and avoids payment of substantial moneys for a down payment or full payment in cash. The leasing company may not insist upon much money "up front," but instead will settle for a long-term payout at a favorable rate of return. In return for this favorable rate, the leasing company continues to own a marketable piece of hardware at expiration of the contract. The third-party lease does remove the responsibility of hardware disposal for the owner. In all probability, your data processing needs will continue, and you will be faced with the necessity of securing new equipment or negotiating a new lease. With a lease, you do not have the problem of re-selling your used equipment if you decide to make a hardware change.

If at the end of the contract you elect to keep the equipment, you may not have much leverage for negotiation resulting in a lower rate. The leasing company can inform you, quite honestly, that other companies are paying a higher rate. This might serve as a notice for you to include purchase options in the original contract. There are so many options including lease and purchase of each peripheral unit, it may be difficult to put together a financial arrangement wholly beneficial to you, the user. It can be done, but only if you attempt to structure the total package for your benefit, possibly paying a premium for desirable options.

Summarizing Equipment Buy or Lease Decisions

As in writing a program or making a business decision, there is not a lone solution to the question. Even if you omit the factors discussed above, you must also consider attitudes of management concerning buying or leasing. Some managements still believe IBM only leases, never selling equipment. This management may also refuse to sign a long-term lease for a computer but will lease a building for ten years, with additional five-year options.

This confusing display of options should be considered as opportunities or challenges. Rather than worry about selection of options and choices, you should take notice of flexibility found in these options. It would not be unreasonable to visit a shop and learn whether the DP manager is making all available use of every described option, including some not mentioned in this text. No single rule fits all companies in all situations. Some of these decisions and options may be beyond your authority, but actual choice of the equipment and expected useful life is of paramount concern to you. Your strongest recommendations for the future will have a noticeable effect on management decisions to lease, buy, or leave things in your capable hands. The financial decision may be out of your control but does not relieve you of responsibility to make all recommendations for the good of the company.

If these decisions are beyond your present level of competence, you would be advised to learn about return on investment, cost of money, resale value for used computers, investment tax credit, etc. By so doing, you exercise tighter control over your installation and gain valuable knowledge of financial factors involved in managing an entire business. (See recommended reading in the appendix.)

Review Questions

1. Be prepared to discuss the various means of equipment leases, with pros and cons for each.

2. As equipment ages, the cash value tends to decline. Is this justification for a constant cycle of purchasing and resale as new products are announced?

3. If your employer is not in a period of rapid growth, discuss the use of purchasing as a means of reducing equipment costs.

4. After the first 176 meter-hours of usage, hourly rates for use of the equipment drop rather dramatically. What are some of the problems facing a manager in going to a two- or three-shift operation? Is the decreased equipment cost sufficient to warrant added costs of personnel and supervision?

5. Maintenance expenses are included in monthly lease costs and are priced separately on purchased equipment. Do these charges adequately reflect the costs of hardware maintenance?

chapter 6

Managerial Planning for the DP Function

You, as DP manager, are faced with the traditional functions of management: planning, organizing, and controlling. Staffing duties may also be included if your shop is large enough to justify a logical separation of duties and delegation of responsibilities. In addition, you may assume extra duties of a purchasing agent, interviewing vendors marketing forms, accessories, and other consumables used in your operation. In the smaller organization, these tasks are usually handled by the DP manager because company purchasing departments may lack the necessary expertise to make purchasing decisions for data processing.

Functionally, your position is management. You have assumed the role for many reasons—those of management and for your own personal reasons. A manager is expected to be effective in assuming all duties that go with the job. Your immediate chore is to define the job, its duties, and means through which you will accomplish your goals. To do this, it is imperative that you plan ahead. A plan can be short- or long-range and ill-defined. Planning to achieve your goal is a difficult task at best. This is not acceptable as an excuse for not planning at all. A strategy, though ill-defined, is certainly more desirable and usable than no scheme at all. The following topics should be of value in overall planning for your installation.

Job Descriptions

A small organization may not be fortunate enough to have a personnel department to function like textbook versions. If your installation is relatively new, there may be no written job descriptions, no job standards, and no minimum requirements for hiring. If this situation exists, you should seize the opportunity to write your own job descriptions and establish minimum hiring and staffing requirements. Figures 3 and 4 illustrate such examples.

The examples shown are very good, but not very exciting reading. However, requirements are clearly spelled out in such detail as to allow a skilled interviewer leeway in screening. The personnel department should perform these functions, with ultimate hiring decisions reserved for you. If a job description does not fit your exact requirements, at least it will provide a base for adaptation to exact needs.

Job functions vary widely with types of organizations, and your internal positions will be no exception. Your own job description should spell out, in detail, lines of authority and responsibility. Justification for this is simple. You cannot perform your assigned role effectively unless you are made aware of what is reasonably expected from a data processing manager. Even if you write your own job description, you will be putting together a list of functions and duties to contribute to success.

Figure 3: Sample Job Description
Manager of Data Processing

Plans and directs all data processing activities of the corporation. Plans for improvements to the corporation's activities through new or improved systems. Directs the fulfillment of data processing services, development, and production. Through liaison with users of data processing services, provides support for improving organization activities through improved methods and techniques and better utilization of resources. Organizes data processing resources to provide efficient and effective service to users.

Source: Data Processing Division, International Business Machine Corporation, *Organizing the Data Processing Activity.*

Figure 4: Sample Job Description
Class A Programmer

Works independently or under only general description on complex problems which require competence in all phases of programming concepts and practices. Working from diagrams and charts which identify the nature of desired results, major processing steps to be accomplished, and the relationships between various steps of the problem solving routine; plans the full range of programming actions needed to efficiently utilize the computer system in achieving desired end products.

Source: Bureau of Labor Statistics.

This same process should be followed for all personnel employed in the DP shop. The size and diversification of your shop will, of course, determine to some degree what functions are assigned to which people. (If you are THE shop, it is not sufficient to write, "I do it all.") When the staff has reached some degree of size, requiring duties and job functions to be divided among 3–5 people or more, job descriptions are needed for each function. These major functions could be classified as:

1. Management.
2. Operations.
3. Programming.
4. Data Entry.

This simple list is presented only as a guideline and is not meant to be inclusive. Task planning does not cease with preparation of your internal job descriptions. This skeletal outline provides an operative framework for setting internal goals and objectives.

DP Goals and Objectives

It is simplistic to define goals and objectives in terms of football or other sports. Teams scoring the most GOALS win the game and achieve their OBJECTIVE. Goals, therefore, are the mile-markers or guideposts to be passed on the way to meeting or achieving your objectives. As a DP supervisor, one of your easiest tasks will be to formulate short-term goals. Determination of long-range goals is more difficult and must be melded with corporate goals and objectives. Like sand on the beach, you will find goals to be shifting constantly into new patterns.

It may be difficult, but this does not eliminate the necessity of defining goals for your operation. One such example of a goal could be: Data processing shall be charged with the responsibility of supplying management with information and services which will contribute effectively to future success of the organization.

Simple and straight to the point, this definition sets the stage for productive resource usage.

Your assignment is to operate within this framework and make additional delineations of jobs and steps necessary to achieve these ends.

The planning phase will begin with a list of tasks and creation of priorities. Should you first implement accounts receivable, or do prospects of payroll applications offer quick recognizable benefits? Do you automate accounts payable or job costing? These questions defy a ready solution. It may be advisable to have a strategy session with other department heads to do "blue sky" dreaming proposals of this nature which will provide you with necessary lists for tasks envisioned for the future.

Brainstorming sessions also offer the opportunity of attempting to discover additional dividends to be realized through automation. These sessions tend to run wild, get out of hand, and travel far from the original purpose of the meeting. You may come away from the session with planning lists, but no priorities. Other managers may leave the session with the misbegotten idea that you have shouldered their problems and will give their pet projects immediate priority. These brainstorming sessions may break down into side discussions as to how or why such and such a problem will be solved, or why their specific problem is entirely too complex for computer processing. The idea sessions, even considering the disagreeable things that may happen, are nevertheless necessary, and they serve useful purposes. For one thing, a list of proposed tasks is developed in rough form. Secondly, these meetings offer a firm idea of corporate priorities. With these beginnings there is a definite point of origination in setting plans and priorities for the future.

The decision as to actual priorities may not be your responsibility, this prerogative being reserved for a management committee. Before the committee can act, you will be expected to go over the list, separating wheat from the chaff, and prepare a reasonably well thought-out scheme. Some ideas are natural subjects to include on an implementation schedule. Other ideas are by-products from other applications. There are items that will be discarded as not practical. Some feasible ideas will not be practical in terms of costs. Your planning responsibility is to document subjects and be available for later management presentation. In this early stage, there is no need to make an in-depth study. Your advice as manager should be considered, and you may be asked to rationalize planning decisions.

The decision-making process results in a commitment of resources. This is not a decision to be made lightly or hurriedly. A total commitment of available EDP resources is to be made in a balanced fashion, insuring the quickest implementation, without totally disrupting current schedules, nor materially interfering with additional plans beyond the initial project. There are several methods for incorporating new projects into the schedule. One such solution is to examine and accept projects having greatest impact on the company. It may be effective to accept projects that are quick and easy to plan, program, and implement. There are other desirable variations. Some projects must already be in production in order to produce computer output for additional projects. This type of methodical planning has the overall effect of building an internal priority schedule to make full use of computer capabilities.

In a young new shop, emphasis is quite apt to be on traditional applications—billing, inventory control, sales analysis, accounts receivable and payroll. If you are the manager in this enviroment, you should carefully examine the payroll example described below. For shops already in existence, you may skip to the section on sales analysis.

Payroll

Payroll, at first glance, appears to be a rather simple application lending itself to data processing. In reality, payroll accounting is a complicated process in a difficult environment. This situation is composed of the following restrictions:

1. Government restrictions (federal).
2. State taxing authorities.
3. City and county laws.
4. Organized labor agreements.
5. Company policy and philosophy.
6. ERISA.
7. Blue Cross (or similar plans).
8. Many other items applicable to specific situations.

In order for you to write one check for each employee, you have more than a few possibilities that must be considered and included in programming for a payroll:

1. Is the employee officially on the payroll with all forms (tax, union, company, etc.) properly filled out and on file?
2. Is the employee a member of a bargaining group and if so, which one? What are the contract provisions for straight time, overtime, and holiday pay?
3. Is vacation pay due? Did the employee work in this pay period? If so, how many hours? Regular pay, overtime pay, or night premium pay? Are there additional hours of pay due? If so, how is it authorized?
4. Are there any garnishee arrangements?
5. Is this employee hourly? Weekly? Biweekly? Salaried? Confidential executive payroll?
6. Bonus earning for piecework?

This brief list summarizes major requirements. Your payroll programs must include these possibilities and more. Actual calculations of an employee's earnings, taxes, and deductions must include these detailed requirements. Even after the payroll check has been prepared, there are ancillary needs that add many hours to total payroll processing:

1. Internal labor distribution reports and analysis.
2. Certain reports for fringe benefits provided by labor agreements.
3. Various reports of authorized deductions and remittance for these amounts.
4. Monthly, quarterly, and annual reports of taxable wages for local, state, and federal taxing authorities.
5. Seniority lists or rosters.
6. Addresses to be maintained.
7. Other management requirements using payroll data.

When the above items are incorporated in a payroll application, you realize payroll is not just a few simple programs to write registers and checks. Visualize your payroll as each employee representing a sub-office of the corporation. For each sub-office, your requirements are simple. It is your responsibility to keep accurate records on the following office accounts: (1) regular earnings; (2) overtime earnings; (3) holiday pay and accruals; (4) sick pay (used and/or accrued); (5) vacation allowances; (6) tax deduction status (local, state, and federal); (7) authorized deductions (up to ten, possibly twelve); (8) contract or policy allowances for jury duty, funeral pay, etc.; (9) other requirements for your company.

Multiply the accounts for these major headings by the number of employees on your payroll. The total for a 1000-employee organization could be more than 9000 accounts. This will give some idea of the magnitude of payroll problems. This example is used to indicate the extensive programming requirements for what seems to be a simple, straightforward application.

Sales Analysis

The sales manager of your company really participated in a brainstorming session when the topics of sales volume and profitability were discussed. Part of the follow-up session is summarized in the following problem: The sales manager is sincerely concerned with profits and the steps necessary to correct any imbalances. The current sales analysis program calls for data involving sales by each representative, department, and class of merchandise. The sales manager is uncertain of the required effort, but is certain that the data processing department can make available information to make his job simpler and earn greater profits.

Your job will be to analyze facts and present a plan for meeting the needs of the sales manager. In so doing, it is your additional duty to present any additional information valuable to the entire organization. The sales manager's prime concern is with sales; whereas the entire organization must be interested in sales and profits sufficient to meet the payroll and provide stockholders with a reasonable return on investment. Existing files provide little more than salesperson number, department, and dollar volume. On an assumption that sales analysis is high on the priority list, you might proceed along the following lines:

1. Salesman summary by dollar volume—high to low or low to high.
2. Invoice volume distribution—high-volume tickets to low-volume tickets, and number of transactions.
3. A customer analysis indicating customers not buying at the present time. (This is a negative approach with positive benefits.)
4. Customer volume distribution by profit and representative.

There are other variations relatively and easily attainable with existing files. Your job is to include all facets of the organization so you present the following plan to management, designed to meet specific needs of the sales manager *and* the entire organization:

1. Gross profit by item or product. (Is salesman selling only the low-profit items?)
2. A rough forecast of production needs. (Refinement of production forecasting should be scheduled as a project for later in the system cycle.)
3. Customer profitability. (Evaluate customers who contribute to sales, little to profit.)
4. A listing for the credit manager of customers and their activity. (It does little good for the salesman to sell a customer with a bad credit history.)
5. The purchasing department may use the above information in determining raw materials to purchase for anticipation of future needs.
6. Personnel may be interested in staffing requirements based on sales and production forecasts.

Very simply and easily you have created a process utilizing information available from different sources to meet many needs. The information is available in rough form from several sources. Your job is to organize and present this information. Presenting this information is more than a simple schedule for report distribution.

The real presentation is made when you sell the use of this information to various department heads. The manager of a department must be made aware of the potentially valuable information included in a report. You have the opportunity to instruct this person in effective use of this information, because if information is not utilized, you have wasted expensive time and materials, receiving nothing in return. The "selling" of data is a very important function, so important that you cannot assume a department manager to be aware of the potential value of reported information. Your presentation to the sales manager must be made in an understandable language—sales and profits.

Summary

The old adage—plan your work and work your plan—is more than a truism. Planning is the essence of success in any job. Time spent in planning "up front" is more than amply rewarded in the successful completion of a project that meets and exceeds planned design requirements. Basic job descriptions are useful in determining manpower requirements necessary to complete the assigned tasks. The task also requires detailed planning on your part to enable the DP department to present data in a useful fashion. The application examples present a brief picture of complexity and detailed planning that may be required for utilization of stored data. The success of your applications and machine utilization will be affected seriously by planning. Do your planning. It pays off in user satisfaction.

Planning functions, as described in this chapter, are simple. In practice, decisions for goals and objectives are not made so readily. The planning involved at this point is basic and functional. The planning examples discussed earlier are meant to show long-range effects of DP-supplied information on the enterprise. More detailed planning will be discussed when we consider the managerial role.

Review Questions

1. What is the difference between goals and objectives?
2. What is the prime goal of data processing?

3.   In selecting an application for automation, you find that there are some applications which offer long-range benefits; others are short-range in nature. All represent significant opportunities for cost reduction and the enhancement of data processing. If the decision is solely left to your own discretion, which (short- or long-range benefits) would you select, and why?

4.   Name some pitfalls of brainstorming when used as a planning technique.

5.   In making a commitment of resources, you are setting a schedule for completion. Are there good reasons for not committing all resources to a single project?

6.   Payroll and sales analysis applications were discussed in this chapter. In your opinion, which of the two offers the greatest potential for corporate profit? How would you maximize benefits from the less profitable alternative?

chapter 7

Data Entry

To be acceptable for processing, raw data must be converted into media suitable for computer input. A DP manager must be knowledgeable concerning equipment available for entry of data. Each method possesses certain unique properties and suitabilities for many applications. There are also built-in restraints for each method. As a manager, you should be concerned with the following list of possibilities:

1. Punched paper tape.
2. Punched cards.
3. Diskettes.
4. Key-to-tape (disk).
5. Cathode ray tubes.

Profitable possibilities are contained in each option. Your choices are limited only by defined needs and potential applications.

Paper Tape

Paper tape continues to be used as a recording media in many installations. Very simply, by punching holes in a continuous paper tape, it is possible to record data for later transmission into a receiver. Paper tape, as input media, is relatively low in cost. Punching equipment (such as a Teletype) is slow, reliable, and inexpensive. The operation does not require a high degree of technical competence for operations. Once recorded in punched holes, data remains usable until the tape is shredded from repeated processings. Some commercial users have coupled the tape punch with an adding machine, or a ledger card accounting machine, to produce tape as a by-product of extending and accumulation of totals.

Paper tape has built-in limitations of physical capacity and speed for today's technology, but there is a definite place for paper tape in data preparation. It is lacking in sophistication but continues to offer utilitarian functions that are cheap and simple. There are IBM system 7's still using paper tape as an effective method of loading established programs. (Paper tape is not recommended for program patches.) In most commercial installations, paper tape has been supplanted by other methods possessing significant advantages without the disadvantages of bulky paper tape reels.

The Punched Card

The familiar "tab" card containing 80 columns of recorded information has seen many changes since Mr. Hollerith introduced his first equipment. There have been cards with 45, 51, 80, 90, and 96 columns. The 80-column cards are oldest in terms of service and usage. The popularity of the 80-column card is declining, but it remains a viable method for recording data.

Cards may be considered old-fashioned—indeed, they are old— but they possess some superior qualities over other forms of processable media. A card may be held in the hand for visual verification. A card may readily be filed (or misfiled, as the case may be) or destroyed at will. Information is instantly available, and with reasonable maintenance, a card will remain processable for years.

The 96-column card, designed for System 3 users, represents a major attempt to enhance the value of card processing. One large advantage is obviously the addition of 16 columns for a 20% increase in capacity. The code structure is simple, easy to read and understand. The punched holes are almost pinpoint in size, and in a radical departure from the 80-column format, are round. The smaller size, roughly one-third that of the conventional card, requires considerably less filing space. Cost is not exactly proportional to size, but freight bills are proportionately reduced. Twenty thousand of the small cards are shipped per case; whereas the conventional case holds 10,000 cards and weighs about fifteen pounds more.

Advantages of any style or size card for processing are as numerous as the disadvantages. Cards can get lost, folded, and mutilated. Card I/O equipment is electromechanical, requiring increased time and higher costs for maintenance. In addition, card gear is considered slow when measured in electronic terms. The "cardless" configurations have managed to operate in an environment bypassing the conveniences of cards, but bear in mind there *are* occasions when a card is more flexible in usage than any other media.

Diskettes as Magnetic Media

The diskette is a comparative latecomer to the data processing scene. The so-called "floppy" diskette is a relatively inexpensive method for the recording and storing of limited amounts of data. The recording capacity is extremely large in relation to physical size and weight. The stated maximum number of records that can be stored on one side of a conventional diskette is 1,898 records. Each record may contain up to a maximum of 128 characters of information. When considering the cost benefits of "floppy" diskette input against card costs and handling, the diskette is far more desirable.

Information may be stored for an indefinite period of time, and a diskette may be used almost continuously for months or years. Several data sets (files) may be defined and stored on one diskette. Users are also required to furnish a transmission device between computer and keystation. Transmission times are slow (in electronic terms) but are extremely reliable, cost-effective, and much faster than comparable card readers.

This method of data entry offers many additional advantages over card input. An equivalent of more than 2,000 punched cards will weigh a very few ounces and may be filed in a conventional letter file. They may be mailed, or transmitted, over long distances. After sustained periods of processing, a diskette may lose some degree of reliability for continual processing and should be replaced. Net benefits of diskette processing are very favorable. It is a method easy to implement, inexpensive, and requires only minimal amounts of program modification and practically no operator training.

This method can also be considered as a transitional device to be used between card punching and the eventual introduction of CRT's or other key-to-tape methods.

Key-to-Tape (Disk)

Key-to-tape disks are key-driven devices, which offer notable advantages over cards and diskettes. The unit-record (card) concept which was effectively advanced by the diskette is virtually bypassed with key-to-tape processing. Tape or disk offers the user almost unlimited record lengths and increased flexibility for mixing several tasks on a tape. Numbers of programming levels are increased, and extensive provisions for supervisory control are included. Particularly suitable for high-volume jobs, key-to-tape has the added benefit of combining many jobs on one or more reels of tape. If the number of jobs is relatively high and job volume is low, these devices may lose some operational effectiveness. This loss is caused by requirements for operator intervention.

As technology moves forward, the control center has become a small CPU, providing powerful capabilities for file or table lookup and extensive edits. The central station brings computing power closer to user levels and frees the main CPU for more productive tasks.

In addition, by being a stand-alone device, key-to-tape systems may be geographically dispersed. In the event of mainframe hardware malfunctions, stand-alone devices do not suffer any performance degradation. On-line tubes are part and parcel of the mainframe, subject to CPU failures and programming problems.

Cathode Ray Tubes

The cathode ray tube (CRT) may be a terminal on-line to the central computer. Other key-driven terminals are available without the video display tube. For example, terminals without video display are found at some airline terminals and may have the capability of printing airline tickets. The CRT makes computing power available to a host of users quite literally at the touch of a key. For the user, a CRT offers true computing power with this power extended into, and made a part of, data entry.

Under strict programming control, the terminal operator may have the facility for adding data to existing files, deleting selected data, updating and changing records, and ability to inquire into file or record status without affecting data. This is not to be considered batch processing though the terminals are frequently used for batch data entry. Using CRT's for data entry, in batch or on-line mode, does provide an operator with extensive edits, validity audits, limited arithmetic calculations, and range checking at point of entry. This is accomplished with computer resources and eliminates the need for machine-readable media as an intermediate step in processing.

Usage of CRT's affords a basic decentralization of the data entry function with no significant loss of control. You can make data available to the end-user in a few seconds without the print-time normally associated with providing information. Terminals, like other methods of data entry, are still another choice to be made by the manager. Your decision should be a reflection of the needs and urgencies of the installation. For example, choosing the on-line CRT indicates a pressing need for instant information. In this case, other factors have become subordinate.

Data Collection Systems

Data collection systems, such as the IBM 5230, bring elements of data entry to originating source. This power at shop or warehouse level may reduce notably the need for repeated transcribing and processing of documents to record transactions after occurrence. Data collection systems lend themselves to operations with a high number volume of transactions, each transaction requiring limited amounts of input. These systems do not obviate the need for data editing and auditing. Validation requirements for this kind of raw data will be increased due to the diverse skills of users providing system input.

There may be a place for data collection systems in your operation. The front-end costs can be relatively low, and benefits are readily identifiable.

In making elemental computing power available at the lowest user level, you will tend to reduce key entry requirements, making data collection and recording a byproduct of non-DP operations. This can be an effective trade-off. It is cost-effective to substitute computing power for key-driven machines and operators. Additional computer time may be needed for validating large amounts of data which, in turn, may provide additional management information.

Data Entry Summary

The many options discussed above for data entry are not meant to be inclusive. No discussion was devoted to mark-sense cards, optical mark, or character readers, or terminals using magnetic tape casettes. These last-mentioned options are available to the user in situations extending beyond the traditional data entry function. In some instances, these other methods may be much more adaptable for your needs. (Bob Laurentz, an IBM SE formerly in the Houston office, was quite fond of responding to all questions concerning applications with this stock statement—"Well, it all depends" . . . .)

In your situation, it all depends.

Data entry is, or can be, a labor-intensive appendage to your computer installation. If a need for additional keystations is developing, you should consider total costs for additional operator stations. Economies of space may be realized by operating a multi-shift shop. These economies may be offset by additional costs for supervision and security.

Since data entry can be expensive, you must stay informed about the many available options. A careful, studied approach of option mixing and matching for profit may result in a greater utilization of machine and human resources. Decisions concerning the data entry function need not be considered as "locked-in." Future needs of the business will require your decisions to be constantly re-evaluated to take advantage of newly developed techniques. Data entry, unlike other functions of an installation, requires a high degree of careful, detailed attention.

Some managers may tend to neglect the importance of data entry. This should be considered the grossest of mistakes. A supply of accurate data is required to keep your CPU producing information in an effective manner. If you are operating, or planning to, in a decentralized data entry environment, bear in mind that responsibility for data entry cannot be wholly delegated to other departments. You are responsible for all data processing tasks, regardless of form and location.

Review Questions

1. List the various methods for data entry.

2. Describe a situation when or where the most expensive form of data entry is required. Give an example of circumstances requiring a less expensive alternative.

3. Data collection devices offer a convenient method of entering data into the mainstream of data processing. What are some limitations and restrictions?

4. In adding a staff member to data entry, what are the additional cost factors?

5. Key-to-tape and key-to-disk devices are potentially powerful devices for storing and editing large quantities of data. For the small user, what are the limitations and restrictions? Name some "hidden costs" not included in the price of these auxiliary devices.

chapter 8

Data Entry Planning and the Future

For the small system user, tubes and workstations have been relatively expensive and not always applicable for or in the small installation. As hardware costs decrease with increasing technology, more and more systems are moving to a workstation concept. A workstation may be considered to be a powerful addition and enhancement to the data entry function. It would be a mistake to utilize this concept without a careful evaluation of the implications for spreading "computer tentacles" throughout the office. Early in the installation planning stage, you may wish to make allowances for including workstations in the future.

In implementing the concept of computing power residing on desks throughout the organization, there will be at least five steps before the project can be completed. These steps are:

1. Planning.
2. Training and indoctrination.
3. Transitional phase.
4. Final implementation.
5. Status review.

You should embark upon the planning stage slowly and carefully. The impact of CRT's and workstations on user departments can be devastating. There is a different approach for the satisfactory resolving of the problems before the equipment is ordered. This method will put the concept into immediate stages of training and indoctrination. By utilizing this idea, you will minimize the effect upon the user and increase your own effectiveness. For older established installations, it is not a revolutionary concept. To the younger manager, it may represent a divesting of control.

In reality, the theory of decentralized data entry is a valuable management tool which will improve operations in all user departments.

Transitional Keystations

The IBM 3741 and 3742 are excellent transitional devices, filling a gap between traditional card punches and CRT's. A limited screen exists displaying data and message prompting. (Prompting messages are available only on the 3741.) The machine is quiet; keyboard and touch are similar to a typewriter; and for the unskilled user, there are no error cards to be extracted from the stacker and scrapped. Operations and instructions are quite simple, and beginning operators are readily trained, achieving quite satisfactory production rates with a minimum of training.

To justify a data entry device in the user departments, there must be sufficient workloads and applications to justify assignment of an operator *and* equipment dedicated to single department use. Once this hurdle has been passed, the rest of the plan may be put in motion. For most user departments, the 3741 is quite satisfactory; though work volumes may dictate additional keyboards. In the beginning, it is wise to start with small and simple applications, highly repetitive in nature. Your department must supply training and a goodly amount of "hand-holding" expertise. A qualified staff member should be assigned to this training phase—probably not the best data entry operator, but one of the best employees in the department. Careful attention to training needs at this point will create a successful operation in the user department.

User-prepared entries produce better data for processing than a highly trained staff. Where the entire computer operation may get blamed for everything from sunspots to acne, a department supplying prepared data for the computer will take great pride in job accomplishment. This pride in achievement should be praised and mentioned throughout the organization. Where your own data entry operators are the best in the business, they tend to regard each assignment as just another job to do and do well. User departments, being involved with actual input data, tend to take greater pride in work preparation and in meeting internal schedules.

In selecting this course for decentralized data entry, be methodical and careful in adding these operations and decreasing your internal capabilities for data entry. The wisest move is to begin with simpler applications in a department, prove success of the plan, and proceed carefully into the next application. In all probability, your department may be held responsible for a continuing training function. This is the opportunity to ensure that all operators are well trained and skilled in meeting job requirements. The distribution of work and machines will have quite a noticeable effect upon budget and staff. This will allow you to concentrate upon more pressing duties for utilizing mainframe power and planning for future implementation of workstations or tubes.

With valuable experience and knowledge gained from interfacing with several user departments, you will find it relatively easy to offer a new, more powerful device to simplify input data preparation. The new devices have greater prompting facilities, and serve as a closer link between user and computer. As users grow in experience and knowledge, requests for additional applications and information will flow even faster.

Decentralization of data entry via 3741's is only a waystation on the route to installation of workstations supported by true computing power. The task of indoctrinating and training user department personnel is made easier by progressing through several phases of careful implementation if this transitional period is to be allowed to gain departmental acceptance. By making your mistakes early, and learning or profiting from them, the final conversion should be made simpler.

Review Questions

1.   What steps are to be taken in the decentralization of data entry?

2.   Discuss pros and cons for decentralizing data entry by the use of user department operators and equipment.

3.   Why is the 3741 (or 3742) considered to be a transitional device?

4.   User departments frequently are not accustomed to stringent requirements for data input and entry. How would you ease the training in these departments?

chapter 9

Security

From days of the Trojan horse through Nathan Hale, Mata Hari, the OSS, CIA, and including the fictional James Bond as Agent 007, the subject of information security has been of prime concern to military leaders, especially in time of conflict. With advent of the Industrial Revolution, industrial espionage became a potent weapon for commercial enterprises to use against one another. More recently, electronic aids such as wireless microphones and concealed tape recorders or wiretapping have helped to create security measures as a way of life. Security measures do not end with electrified gates, closed-circuit TV, or controlled-access doors. To be effective, precautions begin far beyond the physical perimeter and terminate inside the computer complex.

True horror stories abound concerning disgruntled employees or an ex-employee who deliberately sets about to destroy files and procedures. Accidental destruction of data is only one hazard of managing an installation. Deliberate acts, designed to produce monetary loss, are even more frightening to contemplate. No existing system has yet been found to be totally secure against danger from within or without.

Regardless of implied risks, the DP installation is involved in security precautions and must take steps to minimize exposure. Security procedures for your installation do not necessarily involve an impregnable system. Certain minimum precautions should be taken to eliminate or reduce reasonably foreseeable hazards. If your shop is high on a hilltop or mountainside, there may be little or no danger from flood; but rock falls and mud slides may present other perils. Down in a valley, presence of a river may indicate flood possibilities. (There was a major installation located in an office building basement. At a security meeting and seminar the manager realized with a sense of horror the floor had no drains of any sort. No fire—no flood—hazard, but what would happen if pipes on an upper floor froze and burst? During the next coffee break, the manager called headquarters and took immediate action to correct this oversight.) Natural disasters of fire and flood are relatively easy to forecast and possibly measure in terms of hazardous circumstances.

In the small company, general security measures are frequently ignored or shoved aside as being unnecessary. This fallacy is hard to destroy. There are physical aspects of security such as protection against natural disasters. A corporation, being a legal entity, is obligated to guard against theft of money or information such as patented processes, etc. In providing for security, you must also be aware of the dangers involved in personnel—past, present, and future employees.

It is not necessary to call in an ex-FBI agent or veteran of Air Force security services to survey the situation and make recommendations for protecting Fort Knox. These "types" may have little concept of data value as an item to be secured. Nor do you need an overly strict "cops and robbers" approach to dictate needs and responses. You will need a common sense approach and reasonable checkpoints to establish minimal precautions.

The small corporation may exist without formalized security procedures. Your installation *can* get by without a formal set of rules and guidelines. This will not negate the need for security; it only provides a starting point. (If your company does not believe in security, ask why doors have locks.) For internal satisfaction and computer room discipline, you would do well to establish formal steps and procedures necessary to establish a modicum of security.

There are established internal control points and procedures in general use through, and across, industry lines. Ask your auditors to furnish guidelines and their recommendations for establishing internal controls. The accounting profession has many publications which may be used as a reference to reduce or eliminate potentially dangerous procedures. Some controls should be considered as fundamental to accounting and even more desirable for data processing.

The more familiar classes of internal controls include:

1. Separation of duties: Personnel who usually write checks should not have check-signing authority or responsibility, nor should they be allowed to reconcile the same back accounts.

2. Formal job assignments and vacation procedures: All employees without exception are required to take vacations. Where feasible, employees should be shifted, or rotated, between job assignments.

3. Internal controls: Checkpoints and balances should be established and maintained by different employees. (This point is discussed in detail in another chapter.)

4. Formalized control of DP programs and libraries: A definite scheme to formalize access to programs and data is highly desirable.

Of the four items mentioned above, only one is concerned with the internal technical workings of an installation. The other three items are basic and fundamental accounting-type controls; however, their application to electronic processing is also basic.

Data security is a problem that bears only generally on physical security. Internal accounting controls and personnel procedures are designed to establish responsibility for transactions as they progress through normal channels. Data security is much more complex and costly than certain aspects of physical security.

Physical Security

Physical security involves some basic items for management evaluation and concern, such as: (1) file backup and off-premises storage; (2) emergency recovery procedures; (3) hardware backup; (4) fire and natural disasters; and (5) man-made problems.

It is possible to consider the general topic as emergency planning, and this would not be an unreasonable assumption. To play the game, you could ask yourself, What happens if? Or you could ask an outsider how to best put your shop out of operable commission. These two answers would provide an interesting framework and point of departure for establishing a security plan in your shop.

Of these items, file backup and off-premises storage offer the greatest return for least dollar investment. Omitting other considerations, this one step would enable the installation to function (on a reduced basis, perhaps) after occurrence of any major disruption. Formal backup procedures should be integrated into the daily operation of your shop. Time required for copying files is minimal. Additionally, backup procedures are a "must" in preventing accidental losses of data or files during normal processing.

From simple backup procedures, it is a short step to establishing and maintaining backup files at a safe storage point removed from the installation. There is a certain amount of discipline involved in establishing these formal procedures. This controlled discipline produces benefits by reducing, if not eliminating, the threat of an entire file being lost or destroyed by any means.

Emergency recovery is made much simpler if backup procedures are in existence and being enforced. In preparing data and files for storage, do not overlook storage of runbooks and operating procedure manuals. In some types of emergencies, your operating personnel may be incapacitated. Without some form of detailed instructions for machine operation, prospects for recovery may be dimmed considerably. It is a difficult enough process to keep operating instructions on a current basis, much less in an emergency situation; it is truly a disaster not to have *any* operating instructions available.

In discussing backup for hardware, you may assume your machine to be exactly like every other mainframe bearing a like series number. But this is not often the case. There are more than subtle differences in core, system generation, availability of a card reader or a diskette device, printer capacity and print styles, plus variations in peripheral devices such as disk capacities and tape densities.

IBM is very efficient in establishing a backup facility, though you may discover major machine differences when actually faced with a real emergency situation. In our discussion of relations within the DP community, we suggested establishing an informal working relationship and backup provisions in case of emergency. In so doing, be very much aware of the changing configurations to be found in many installations. You should also be prepared to reciprocate in kind by furnishing backup hardware for another company or installation. There are companies and organizations who are reluctant to enter into a backup arrangement without a formal agreement. This protects both parties against changes of personnel and corporate policy. With or without the formal agreement, it is your duty to establish and maintain emergency backup procedures.

Fire and Natural Disasters

Certain physical limitations dictate planning for a flood, caused by rising water or as a result of hurricanes or tornadoes. If a river with flooding potential is nearby, provisions would also refer back to and include allowances for a continuation of operations. Hurricanes and similar weather disturbances are not so predictable. Nevertheless, emergency precautionary measures should be planned for implementation in the event of an impending disaster. As a matter of good practice, it would be an excellent test of capabilities to simulate (estimate high water levels) a flood, or high water. The lessons learned from the exercise would be used to refine existing plans.

Fires are not so easy to anticipate. The effects of fire may totally disrupt the entire company. In considering the possibility of fire, it is worthwhile to reduce the exposure by installation of fire protection equipment. Some oil refineries and seaports may have their own fire-fighting equipment. Offices may elect to provide other optional equipment for control and the extinguishing of fires. These items have a definable cost and are effective in minimizing damages as a result of fires. One of the simplest devices is a heat-sensitive alarm which emits an audible alarm and alerts personnel who are in the immediate area. For this device to be efficient, it should be wired in to a system which will notify fire department or security personnel. These systems must be reasonably tested on a scheduled basis. The smoke alarm operates in much the same fashion and is particularly valuable in detecting smoldering sources of smoke.

For the computer room, several fire-fighting devices are readily available on the commercial market. Each extinguishing agent is most effective when used as recommended by the manufacturer or insurance agent. Most hand-held extinguishers are labeled with specific instructions for use on different types of fires. Complete fire control systems are designed for an entire building, or perhaps just the computer complex. Before electing the apparently most economical approach, you should consider some extinguishing agents and their use in a data processing environment.

For smoldering wood and paper fires, perhaps water is the most widely used. Water is cheap, readily available, and effective when used correctly. It is not desirable, nor effective, to use water in an attempt to control and/or extinguish electrical fires. Water is a conductor of electricity and does nothing to remove the source of the fire. Electrical fires usually have a source of heat that must be eliminated before the fire can be extinguished.

Another old standby is the familiar soda and acid device. This is a mixture of soda which combines with an acid substance, producing a foam-type mixture which removes oxygen from the immediate area. It is very effective for some small office-type fires. When used on electronic equipment, it does leave a residue that is difficult to remove.

The CO_2 extinguisher is very useful for containing fires in a small area. By removing oxygen from the source of heat, the fire is virtually smothered. Carbon dioxide leaves no harmful effects on the equipment. For a large area, a CO_2 system is very effective as a fire-suppressant. Unfortunately for the personnel in this space, it will also make the area totally insupportable for humans by removing oxygen. Additionally, if electronic components are cooled too much, this may lead to the spreading of an electrical fire by conducting electricity.

HALON, a fire-suppressant agent in gaseous form, is perhaps the most effective for fire control inside a relatively sealed computer complex. There are no harmful residues, and it offers some protection for personnel who are in the immediate vicinity of a fire. HALON is recommended very highly by some casualty insurance companies for some very specific needs. A total system using HALON is effective, but not the cheapest type available. If recharging the system becomes necessary, be prepared to pay a relatively expensive price.

System Summary

In mentioning a few of the readily available types of fire-extinguishing systems, we have barely mentioned cost considerations. Nor have we discussed to any degree the merits and disadvantages of each system by comparison with another. Requirements for an effective system should be discussed with top management and a representative from the casualty insurance company. As a manager, you should be aware of the various types and amounts of protection available.

Case Study 1

As recently appointed manager of the GeMeEe installation, you have been asked to make a survey for physical security requirements and report back to the firm president. In addition, you know the president will also expect recommendations for choosing a course of action.

Assumptions: This is a manufacturing concern employing 460 employees, including a data processing staff of 13. No other assumptions.

Assignment 1: Be prepared to discuss merits and disadvantages of various fire extinguishing systems.

Assignment 2: Prepare a separate list of recommendations for physical aspects of security (door locks, buzzers, closed-circuit TV, guards, etc.).

Assignment 3: Recognizing that some items are prohibitive, prepare your list for the president in three sections:

1. Absolutely minimal requirements.
2. Reasonably adequate coverage.
3. No expenses spared.

Assignment 4: Prepare a brief outline of an internal security manual for your staff.

Case Study 2

In an effort to minimize costs and provide basic elements of fire and data security, you have been requiring the operator to back up files on a weekly basis and store them at home. Last night in a fit of anger, the operator "scratched" all master files and left for parts unknown. This morning you discovered the disaster.

Assignment 1: Describe the risks taken in the situation outlined above. Be prepared to discuss errors of omission and commission

Assignment 2: What are your recommendations for avoiding a similar disaster?

Assignment 3: Write a memo to the company president describing the incident. Omit nothing from the memo.

Assignment 4: How are you going to recover from this situation?

chapter 10

Functional Position of a Data Processing Department

Beyond the merely technical problems of a computer installation are real questions of management philosophy concerning placement in the organizational charts of the data processing function. The usual scheme for separation of line and staff duties does not fit most situations involving the DP installation. With a role crossing many departmental lines of authority and responsibility, a computer complex presents a different mix of challenges and opportunities. Office automation offers distinct possibilities for potential cost reductions. The effect of electronic automation will have a significant impact on general office procedures. Information generated through these techniques will be a major factor in setting many corporate policies and procedures. The ideal role for an installation would include a complete integration of line, staff, and more importantly, computer functions. The inherent benefits of this type of organization can best be realized when full utilization is made of all electronic capabilities.

Efficient handling of data becomes a problem of major proportions as a business organization increases in size. In order to maintain or improve a competitive edge in the marketplace, efficient application of computer techniques offers some of the best prospects for cost management. Dr. Beckman expressed this idea from a broader management viewpoint when he said: "Essentially management has to do with the most effective and economical use of all factors of production and their component parts in the accomplishment of the organization's objectives, the main one of which is that of producing a desired output."

[1]Dr. T. N. Beckman, "The Value Added Concept as a Measurement of Output," *Advanced Management*, April 1957, p. 6.

In considering organizational placement of the installation, we should consider additional aspects of computer planning. The construction of a blueprint for an organization to meet future socio-economic challenges is a function of management that cannot be delegated; nor more importantly, ignored. The question of placement embraces problems of such magnitude as to demand the highest degree of personal attention and consideration from top management. Unfortunately, this is usually not the case.

Corporate management may be very much aware of the capabilities of a computer in performing prodigious numbers of mathematical computations in easing clerical workloads. However, development and integration of a computer installation into an existing corporate structure is a slow, laborious task. Simultaneously, this task must remain in step with the management process. Otherwise, it may outstrip current management concepts and suffer a possible loss of support. Or, if DP development lags behind planned performance, credibility of the manager and installation may be called into question.

From the viewpoint of consistency, all accounting functions belong under jurisdiction of the accounting department in the same manner in which production functions belong to a production manager. In this case, you should examine the role of a computer objectively and determine whether it is a staff or line function, or is a service department meeting organic needs of management across departmental lines.

DP Line Functions

Payroll, labor distribution, accounts receivable and payable, and cash flow projections are logically grouped (loosely) under the accounting or controller's organization. All of these processes and many more are generally considered to be staff functions though elements of line duties are present. Sales activities require a careful coordination of production and accounting duties and additional items of information to fulfill the role of a line department. The computer can effectively produce all required data for each of the functions named above. This seems to presuppose the EDP task would be relegated to a functional line department. In turn, this would raise additional questions about which operating department should have responsibility for the system.

Can a subordinate function of a line department provide an effective service for other line departments? The answer to this question would appear to be negative, according to one definition of service activities: "Service departments arise from the normal grouping of activities, thus involving the performance of an operating function."[2] If an installation is part and parcel of the accounting department, it is somewhat unreasonable to expect a completely satisfactory series of services to be adequately performed for another department. This violation of traditional line and staff relationships would be unsatisfactory at best. Functional responsibility would as a matter of course be delegated to other departments for determining exact reporting requirements. Problems involving conflict of interest, priority assignment, and cost apportionment are quick to arise when responsibility is diluted. From the factors discussed above, it is logical to draw this conclusion: Responsibility for the DP installation should not be under dual control of one or more line departments.

Staff Functions of EDP

Staff duties by their nature are supportive. In a very limited sense, staff performs the internal *thinking* for an organization. The "line" *acts* for an organization. The principal differences of line and staff are distinguished by authority relationships.

If a staff manager is assigned the reporting responsibility for EDP, this presents other problems to the administrator. A staff manager who is given responsibility for DP concurrently with equal responsibility for another line or staff duty will find himself in an almost impossible management quandary. With no direct control over line functions, a supervisor may be charged with responsibility for accomplishing certain line jobs. This division of responsibility could develop into an intolerable and unworkable situation.

Service Functions

Service departments, the computer installation being a workable example, arise from staff activities which had their beginnings in a grouping of specialized tasks. The importance of the service function will be in direct proportion to its role within the organization. For example, customer engineering at IBM is a direct producer of revenue, but its main

---

[2]Koontz and O'Donnell, *Principles of Management*, p. 172.

function is to keep all machines functioning properly with the least amount of customer inconvenience. The DP complex, as a service function, performs many tasks totally unrelated to a service function or department.

Specialized Requirements

A manager or director of data processing must be a skilled specialist. In addition to these technical skills, a manager must possess intangible conceptual skills allowing the direction of departmental activities in such a way that all internal departmental objectives are directed toward achievement of the corporation's main objectives. The two statements—one mentioning technical skills, the other calling for concepts—are apparently contradictory in nature. First, there is a need for a technician; then there is also a need for an administrator. This paradoxical proposition is not as strange as it appears. Management positions are filled with personnel who began with certain specialized technical skills and rose to positions where conceptual skills are required for the satisfactory job performance.

Full Departmental Status

The functional position of the computer complex within an organization should bear full departmental status; that is, independent of function and reporting to no other line or staff department. Management-assigned duties should be of a service nature, meeting some needs of every operating department. This is the only fashion in which DP is freely allowed to serve the needs of every department. Data processing is a highly specialized activity requiring certain skills and concepts to be applied on an interdisciplinary basis. There are accountants who are well versed in tax matters, others knowledgeable about fixed-asset accounting, and other areas of specialization. Each of them may be required to work with computer-generated output from a (computer) service department who must understand these complexities in addition to bill of materials, accounts receivable, and a multi-state payroll.

If the installation is considered to be a true service unit, there will be other dividends. A production manager in a factory may desire certain reports which an accounting department is unwilling to produce due to limitations of money, staff, and time. This situation could also exist with other line or staff functions. If a service unit is a separate entity, reporting to no single operating department, there will be no interdepartmental conflicts (with DP in the middle). An installation must be productive for the entire organization, even though there are certain departmental tasks requiring large blocks of computer time.

Before advent of the electronic computer, an accounting system was the principal management reporting device. Accounting is a science related to classifying, recording, and summarizing of commercial transactions in monetary terms. Accounting, with a computer, performs more than the mere recordative functions of a "bookkeeper." It becomes a dynamic concept of business reporting.

The relationship of all data within any organizational structure should be an integral part of the management reporting system. More effective controls and checkpoints make data available to management in a much shorter time frame. Planning becomes more of a science than educated guessing. A manager is relieved of the tedious details in directing the efforts of clerks, thus allowing more time for concentration on true managerial tasks. However, the system will always be an aid to management—not a substitute for good management.

Achieving Departmental Status

The preceding section presents a case for establishing the DP department or division as an entity with departmental status, without mentioning the methods for accomplishing or reaching this goal. To achieve this position is not an easy chore. Like many promotions, this position must be earned. There are many instances, such as a life insurance company, where the importance of the department is sufficient to warrant departmental status. There are others where the organization is built around the DP department. For the most part, the early installation is an answer to a specific need of a particular department. Where this is the case, the chances of breaking away and becoming a separate entity are few and widely separated. This is not to deny the possibility, but only to recognize the difficulties involved in a minor (major) corporate reorganization. In this delicate situation, you will be forced to employ your most persuasive skills in convincing management to establish your department as a separate entity.

Dilution of Authority

If the data processing department is an asset to any operating division, that division manager will resist any attempt to dilute, or disperse, his authority by a reduction of responsibilities. This is especially true when the department is successful and thriving with corporate approval and corresponding budget increases. Quite the reverse is true when the installation does not enjoy a position of respect and integrity. Some department heads exist in a little empire, apparently thriving only on size of the budget and not paying adequate attention to management details. In many instances a department leader will only pay court to the operations that are easily understood. The computer, being a strange and unusual animal, may receive scant attention. This situation, though difficult to manage, does present an opportunity for breaking off and establishing a stand-alone computer department or division.

An operating department represents a certain amount of power and authority. An attempt to strip away the symbols and trappings of power is no less than a direct attack upon the leader's authority and will be resisted with much strength and gusto. There should be no direct attack upon the entrenched powers of authority. Nor should you let the situation deteriorate to a point where professional integrity and the status of the department are in question. Rather, the solution may lie in diligent efforts to extend the influence of electronic data processing into so many departments as to create a real need for a separate data processing department. As successful salespersons have known for years, you create a need and then present the solution or answer to fill this created need. To successfully create a department of data processing is a very arduous task, requiring many difficult months or years of hard work and careful managing of talents and opportunities. The task is not impossible, and the end results are extremely desirable from your standpoint as a manager.

Creating the Need

If the computer operation is a necessary adjunct for successful fulfillment of a department's assigned mission, it is even more difficult for DP to achieve departmental stature. Within this framework, it is very difficult to extend DP influence into other areas without prior approval. The task of acquiring additional applications from outside the department will be more difficult.

However, a computer may be compared to a building. The cost of rent, or leasing, goes on whether the building is occupied and in use twenty-four hours a day or whether the equipment is run more than one eight-hour shift. It is relatively easy to justify additional machine applications when hourly machine costs drop dramatically after the first one hundred and seventy-six (meter) hours. This is cost reduction at its finest and is readily applicable in extending the influence of your department. By seizing this concept and utilizing it to the utmost, you may create a 24-hour operation and, incidentally, prepare a strong case for independent activities. Few departmental managers are willing to accept total responsibility for a little-understood operation which may involve other divisions. A lack of operational success will reflect directly upon the department head, causing repercussions through many other levels. Even the most successful of managers will find difficulty explaining away problems caused by losing a printer or master disk files at 2 in the morning. You will probably find the same task just as difficult, but you do understand the problems—and solutions.

In creating this need for independent stature, you may earn something of a reputation for empire-building. There are elements of truth in this, but also many elements of sour grapes. It is not an easy undertaking to satisfy the computing needs of diverse departments and operations. To meet these needs requires detailed understanding of operations and policies far beyond the traditional scope of data processing. Managers not skilled and knowledgeable in the ways of data processing may find it difficult to comprehend requirements of departments unrelated to their own. The usual role of accounting is always separated from engineering and vice versa because there is no common language. The language of a computer must be understood by all parties and should be entrusted to only one master translator—the DP director. The position may be czar-like, but then other department heads occupy a similar position in their bailiwick.

By creating this vacuum for data processing and rushing to fill it, you create internal problems. No other buffer will absorb the slings and arrows of outraged factory workers missing a paycheck, and you may have to explain (to the president) why the inventory is seemingly out of balance or monthly receivable statements were mailed late. Within the same framework, there will be no manager to praise your new programs which reduce machine room labor overtime by 50%, or to recognize the contribution made by a new program reflecting reduction of scrap and increases in production.

With this additional departmental responsibility, there are positive and negative aspects. Rather than being praised for long hours and contributions, these efforts may be ignored and considered a part of the job. The positive aspects may be so small as a reserved parking space and key to the executive restroom.

The increased freedom and professional recognition far outweigh any negative aspects of departmental status. This clearly means a direct assumption of authority and responsibility for your department. Without outside intervention, you have the chance totally to manage the installation and prove the strength and effectiveness of the (your) department.

Review Questions

1.   Based on excellent performance, meeting of production schedules, and a desire for increased job responsibility, you have decided to write a memo to the controller asking for departmental independence. Your memo should be short and concise.

2.   Assume you are the controller for a large organization. Write a brief memo to the DP manager denying a request for departmental status.

3.   Define the distinctions of line, staff, and service functions.

4.   Some elements of DP must of necessity cross departmental lines for authority and responsibility. Will departmental status have any effect upon these lines? If so, why?

5.   Prepare a functional organization chart using your present employer as as a guide. Where would you assign data processing in the event of reorganization?

chapter 11

Managing
the DP Function

Management has not been reduced to a fine art or methodical science. No guaranteed techniques can be applied in particular situations. Managing an installation is directly analogous to management of an enterprise. Like the entrepreneur gathering available resources for potential profit, the DP manager must shepherd and marshal available talents and skills to meet and fulfill the mission of an installation. Specialized needs for data processing are technical in nature, relating only to internal problems involving electronic equipment. By stripping away the esoteric terms inside a machine room, we find computer room management problems to be similar to those of any other supervisor.

Like a conductor of a symphony orchestra, a manager is responsible for staffing (auditioning), training (rehearsal), providing a planned course of action (selecting the music), and production of a product pleasing to top management (audience). There will be scheduling delays, employee absenteeism, machine malfunctions, physical discomforts, and the potential threat of natural disasters. How you respond and address these opportunities will determine your effectiveness as a manager. Proper application of modern techniques for personnel and production management will be of much value in selecting the correct alternatives for success.

Establishing Standards

An installation establishes certain informal standards as a natural outgrowth of the work involved. There is a place for informal levels of performance, but not in the plans for long-range success. It is far more desirable to establish formal standards as an attainable goal and work for their achievement. The use of standards also furnishes a dividend by reducing doubt and confusion regarding job performance considered to be either acceptable or unsatisfactory. It is a comparatively simple task to name and set goals to be achieved. Difficulties lie in implementing these rules as formal procedure and practice. Frequently, the nature of an enterprise will determine satisfactory patterns of performance in addition to previously established informal standards. Criteria for the computer installation must be higher and stricter than those of other divisions in the office structure. A clear understanding and definition of what is considered to be acceptable production will go far in the elimination of doubt and misunderstanding created by flawed instructions. In defining attainable criteria, reasonability and consistency should be the two basic principles.

Internal Controls

Simple implementation of control points tends to enforce a certain level of controlled accuracy as a byproduct. The extra value of logical checks and balances should insure compliance with standard operating procedures. There are various electronic techniques which should be used in the computing process to establish accuracy and validity. It is extremely desirable to include a careful matching and blending of electronic and manual options to produce maximum benefits. Failure to include this duality of interests will tend to degrade effectiveness of the control procedure.

Some items proven valuable in actual practice are:

1. A carefully maintained production log.
2. Checklists of items for inclusion.
3. Time-stamping to record receipts and delivery of work.
4. The function of a control clerk.

The possible delegation of duties to a control clerk does not remove responsiblity for excellent job performance in any department. It remains the duty of a machine room supervisor to create standard operating procedures and insure satisfactory compliance. It is your job to participate in creating these additional job assignments in order to ensure understanding and create the additional machinery required for enforcement. Checkpoints and other control procedures provide the blueprint for defining acceptable levels for satisfactory performance of duties.

Each level of control carries varying elements of cost, and by suggestion, different degrees of effectiveness. There is always the tendency to make a system of checks and balances into a clumsy and cumbersome process of overprotection against all mistakes. In so doing, there is always the possibility of overlooking built-in guideposts. With respect to a process for minimizing errors, there is no process—no matter how expensive, ponderous, or redundant—that will wholly prevent occasional errors from entering undetected into the system. In reducing problems caused by wrong or incomplete data, control costs and potential benefits must be evaluated before a conclusion can be reached. This process will include considerations as to what constitutes an "acceptable risk." The final selection will be based on a combination of decisions weighing alternatives of manageable expenses and studied evaluation of potential losses.

Choices of control techniques will vary from one application program to another. Batch totals are frequently used in addition to batch numbers, and a careful control over numbered documents. Many installations will balance to a predetermined control total or use a form of zero balancing. Under no circumstances should the machine room have responsibility for building *and* maintaining controls. One of the basic accounting principles for separation of function calls for one person to prepare the control; another to maintain balancing in the control ledger. This is especially true for computer processing. Under no circumstances should an operator be allowed to change or alter any control numbers. Controls are the responsibility of the originating department.

A control number may, and probably should, follow all data through subsequent processing. For example, in accounts receivable, daily totals for cash receipts and daily sales must be used in determining net amounts outstanding at the end of an accounting period—weekly, periodic cycles, or monthly. Use of batch numbers for work orders, job requests, or document controls furnishes a reasonable checkpoint or control over work flow through each step.

Hash totals are an arithmetic accumulation of certain numbers not required for processing of the data. This fictitious total may consist of document number accumulations, a summation of account numbers, or even the addition of part numbers. These totals furnish a higher degree of control over all phases of the data. Sometimes hash totals may be used internally to allow greater control of data within the confines of the computer room. There are possibilities of number transposition or omission in the best of shops. If an error in an account number is allowed entry into the processing flow and remains undetected, this one error actually creates two errors. First, it is not where it belongs; and second, it should not be where it is. If the application happens to be accounts receivable, this would make two customers unhappy with their balances—especially when the correcting entries are posted in next month's billing. In financial statement reporting, an error of this nature could be the difference between profit and loss. Control points are beneficial for all departments. They affix some degree of responsibility and set a standard for ready achievement as a normal part of the job procedure.

Building in Electronic Checkpoints

There are many techniques available for building serviceable flags or pointers into every user-written program or procedure. These indicators provide you with a management tool, easy to implement and monitor and at little additional cost in time or materials. The benefits are of measurable value in day-to-day operations.

The creation of a coded structure for programs and applications provides a simple scheme for following a project from inception to completion. The code should be so constructed as to allow for nearly all contingencies. Identification of programs or procedures should be limited to a user-assigned code of six or seven characters. By arranging these characters in a specific pattern, it is possible to identify, and track, all programs and procedures through the department. The first two characters should be designated as identifying the job or application. Numbers or letters may be used, but digits do not lend themselves to mnemonic association; i.e., 24 carries no implication for any specific application, but AR does tend to suggest Accounts Receivable. Using this simple coding scheme, it becomes a logical development and extension to sequentially number all application programs in operating sequence. To carry this idea even further, you may structure the numeric codes to include the extras described in Figure 5.

The built-in facilities of this type structured code allow inclusion of program identification in every report. Whatever scheme of letters and numbers you may adopt should be made a part of almost every program and procedure. (It is not considered good form to print program identification numbers on pre-printed forms such as a payroll check.) If your computer has programmable capabilities for job accounting, a carefully assembled code structure will enable you to implement additional tasks of job costing, machine utilization studies, and possibly even time scheduling. This is an automated process and provides the supervisor with additional information for internal installation control.

Figure 5: Suggested Program Codes

2 Characters	Proposed Numbering
AR Accounts Receivable	Daily 0001 thru 0099
AP Accounts Payable	Weekly 0100 thru 0900
FA Fixed Assets	Monthly 1000 thru 3999
MR Management Reports	Quarterly 4000 thru 4999
GL General Ledger	Annual 5000 thru 5999
SA Sales Analysis	Special 9000 thru 9999
CA Commodity Analysis	
DP Data Processing (internal)	

Program numbering and identification is not just a form of internal eccentricity; it is absolutely vital for maintaining control over the assets of the computer installation. This process serves to differentiate between various types of checks for payroll, expenses, and accounts payable, etc. In striving for this goal of excellence, there may be only a dim light at the end of the tunnel. The simple creation of an organized pattern for standardization will have the overall effect of strengthening corporate and installation policy and aid in enforcing compliance with other standard operating procedures. This will play a significant role in the building of a reputation (internal and external) for excellent job performance.

General Controls and Checkpoints

The choice and usage of controls will vary widely from one application to another. Predetermined totals are used effectively—in and out of data processing. Total tapes for all accompanying documents offer a ready checkpoint, the separation of responsibilities, and they comply with good accounting practices. A control, furnished by a third party, furnishes the computer operator with a balance point which must be met before additional processing can be continued. This basic procedure affixes responsibility at the point of origination and removes the DP operation from total responsibility, if the balance is achieved. This form of discipline is extremely beneficial for every department, as it provides an established number for balance control. There are no circumstances where a computer operation should be considered totally responsible for the quality of input data sent in for processing. It will require the skills of a Disraeli, or a Machiavelli, to earn respect and convince the user departments of the need for established controls. The computer only provides a mirror for the efforts of other departments. Balancing procedures exist to prove that everybody is peering into the same looking-glass.

Standard Form Sizes

If the nature of the enterprise will allow standardization, it is both desirable and economical to select one universal size for all continuous (stock and custom) forms. This is not always possible; however, the number of form sizes should be minimized. Purchasing agreements are thereby easier to negotiate, and inventory requirements are made simpler. The net combination of reduced inventory needs and purchasing agreements should result in a noticeable reduction of forms costs in total. It is a simple task to compare costs of paper stock with those of custom forms. Stock form usage should be emphasized. For general-purpose runs, stock paper offers a low cost (per sheet) even though usage may number thousands of pages, in various combinations of copies and plies. There are just as many options of size and weight as there are variations of so-called "stock" sizes. These choices enable the user to pick and choose the most effective solution. You should be aware that the cheapest source of supply is not necessarily the best. The best source can be measured by costs and service. There are many supply sources for continuous forms, from the small one-man broker to the large international forms manufacturer. The real cost of a form is finally measured in user satisfaction.

As a class, the DP industry tends to follow sheep-like patterns of traditional usage. The reputed industry standard, $14\frac{7}{8}''$ by $11''$ in size, is the most widely used and accepted form in both large and small shops. Using normal heading and overflow spacing, this will allow the printing of 54–58 lines on one page, at six lines per inch (normal typewriter spacing). The size, for the user, is awkward and unhandy. It is not easily bound or filed in any conventional filing cabinet. In an effort to consider efficient utilization, you should give serious consideration to the adoption of another standard size offering increased benefits to the reader and a profitable utilization of computer printing capabilities.

For an effective combination of user convenience and general ease of handling, you would do well to consider the $14\frac{7}{8}''$ by $8\frac{1}{2}''$ depth paper as an installation standard. This is considered a standard by many manufacturers and is warehoused on an "on-the-shelf" basis. These dimensions are almost what is considered to be legal-size. Coupled with eight-lines-per-inch capabilities and a reduced type-font size, this form will reduce the total costs for forms and handling. This can be achieved with no decline in efficiency.

Eight-lines-per-inch (lpi) spacing will present the same number of printed lines on the smaller sheet. The reduced size of print will present a much "tighter" report in terms of physical size. The number of sheets required for a production run may be about the same. This reduced size reduces the need for an extra step of copier reduction and is very easily read. Copying costs will be reduced as there will be little need for a separate process of copying and reducing. If report copies are to be mailed, postage costs will be lowered, and there are no outsize requirements for mailing envelopes. This form is also readily filed in almost any attaché case or briefcase without folding. In addition, there are no costly expenditures for a specialized rack to handle the other size (14⅞" x 11") which was not made for any standard filing system.

Over a period of years, the monetary returns of forms standardization will become apparent. The news section of the May, 1977 issue of Datamation makes mention of a bank that had switched to the smaller stock size and projected annual savings over $100,000. Even IBM is producing some invoices and statements based on the smaller type font and eight-lines-per-inch spacing. If forms are to be mailed, there will be significant savings in postage. Reduced costs for forms handling are not easy to evaluate but are present nevertheless.

The end-user must be given equal consideration when selecting paper sizes and methods for binding. Burst forms are exactly what the name or term implies; these are continuous forms which have been burst into single sheets. On the other hand, unburst forms are still in one long fan-folded stack. Both options offer features which are appealing in actual use. The intended user should be given every consideration when choosing the size of paper and method of binding.

When an unburst report is to be distributed to a user, the more acceptable form of binding is at the top. When opened for use or reference, two pages of printed information are presented to the eye. This presents a possible disadvantage when attempting to read a line on the top printing line of the furthest form. In addition, careless binding could produce a report with no printed pages visible to the reader. Use of a liquid glue binding method will reduce the costs of binding with no loss of access.

Book-like in nature, burst forms should be bound on the side. The finished product occupies the same amount of desk space as an unburst report and yet only presents one page at a time to the reader. Reading is more efficient though there is only one page instantly accessible at any time.

The user will eventually become accustomed to using the finished product from your shop. If your installation is relatively new, it is easy to adopt and set forms standards for the future. For an established installation, it may be more difficult to introduce a new standard. This objection can be overcome by careful attention to, and a comparison of, costs for binding and filing of reports.

The types described earlier are actual examples of forms standardization which have proved their worth in many installations. With attention to detail and the end-user, these suggestions can be readily adapted for use in any installation. In establishing these standards, you may run into opposition from the user departments. This may be a deep-seated reluctance to change, or a plain refusal to consider any new ideas. As with other ideas emanating from the machine room, this may call for a real sales approach complete with a sincere presentation of facts, figures, and estimated benefits.

Review Questions

1. How does DP management differ from that of other corporate functions?

2. What are the difficulties of establishing standards for DP and the entire office structure? Which standards are the most demanding?

3. What are the benefits of mixing manual and electronic checkpoints?

4. Define the role of a control clerk. Should the control clerk be charged with enforcing compliance with standard operating procedures?

5. List some of the limitations and pitfalls in using document controls, batch totals, and other control numbers.

6. Establish a numbering scheme for programs and procedures for each major application area. Describe its application, along with benefits for the installation.

7. Standard forms sizes offer economies to the user and DP departments. Be prepared to discuss and justify your decision in selecting one standard size of stock paper. Present this discussion to the user departments.

8. Prepare a simple example of different styles for binding reports.

chapter 12

Programming Skills
for the Manager

Size and complexity of an installation will determine the amount of programming skills required for a manager. In a System 32 shop, the supervisor may also be the programmer, analyst, control clerk, data entry operator, and in emergencies may be called upon to operate the switchboard. The other extreme in size would the the IBM 370/125 installation. (In this book, the 125 is considered to be at the high end of the small- to medium-size installations.) The 370/125 is usually configured much larger than the ubiquitous System 3, available in so many varying forms. As an installation grows larger and increasingly complex, division of responsibilities is a necessity to fit exigencies of the increased staff size. Generalists—personnel capable of performing many tasks—will be replaced or supplanted by skilled, experienced specialists.

Technical competence required for supervising an installation will decrease as the configuration and staff grow in response to changing needs. There will be needed infusions of additional talents. Mental discipline required for programming is not lost or wasted as the shop grows. This discipline may and should be directed to problem-solving techniques and solutions. Just as a program may be regarded as a problem requiring solution, you may now use programming logic as a technique in solving problems of management and supervision.

Programming knowledge consists of a logical application of skill and experience to the solution of an assigned problem or task. If you consider accounting problems or engineering equations to be exercises in disciplined logic, then you should recognize the challenges and opportunities in applying programming logic to the solution of a problem. If the problem is not one of programming languages or techniques, then the manager must utilize all his acquired knowledge to meet this challenge. Problems of a technical nature, involving production problems, may require a very comprehensive knowledge and understanding of programming. This valuable experience, coupled with management skills, may be needed to assess effectively the complete problem before reaching an effective conclusion or decision.

Your programming skills will decrease in importance, never totally disappearing, as the inherent value of the installation grows. In the smaller shop, every emphasis may be placed on production and throughput, and you may not have the luxury and pleasure of fine-tuning a system for true efficient productivity. Increased installation sizes also require additional time for planning. Prior to this growth, the planning may have been done by another department head or supervisor. The expanding complexity of interrelated programs and applications demands careful attention from the supervisor. Application planning represents an opportunity to forecast and predict the future direction of your installation. This chance for including allowances for future "needs and wants" will bring manifold benefits.

Management demands and requests for increased performance and production may necessitate placing a program in "live" production prior to exhaustive checking and debugging. This will probably result in many reruns and substantial revision of the incomplete programs. This is only symptomatic of myriad and costly losses resulting from inadequate and incomplete planning. Always time to rerun; never time to do it right the first time.

Managerial programming time, lost in the planning phase, is really a net gain of productivity. Planning may not squeeze maximum performance and operating efficiency from a program. Planning will reduce time required in modifying a hastily written program to meet its original stated purpose. Relatively minimal programming techniques can with effort produce a high degree of program and hardware efficiency. Extra efforts to absolutely maximize operating effectiveness may not be economically justified for the small installation. It is quite possible to expend an inordinate amount of programming time and money to achieve miniscule increases in performance. Your managerial skills are better directed toward overall systems improvement rather than saving milliseconds in an infrequently used program or procedure. Managerial success is based on total achievements, not minor improvements for a small piece of the installation.

Supervisory skills required for installation management are quite different from those needed in programming. Whereas management problems encompass a broader range of alternatives, programming tends to concentrate on problem-solving at a functional level. Talents required for programming are effective tools to be used in reaching a conclusion at a relatively low management level. Management problems frequently require a more careful consideration of inter-departmental ramifications. The capable manager considers all options and studies all factors involved, before making a judgmental decision.

Compiler Selections

For the new shop, there is always a problem of selecting a compiler, or various compilers to handle processing loads. A compiler may be defined as an interpreter between man and machine. It converts man-made instructions into suitable form, allowing a computer easy translation into machine language.

Beginning compilers were mostly simple repetitive routines stored in the machine and called forth by the programmer. As the need for productivity increased, stored routines were better defined, expanded, and enriched with computer power. After an extensive development period, a compiler was available with pre-written instructions to be called, or used, by relatively few user-supplied instructions. We may refer to user-written call routines as macros; a macro being a comparatively small set of instructions invoking usage of additional micro instructions in the compiler.

Selecting a compiler involves careful consideration of many possibilities and ramifications. By limiting the installation to single compiler usage, you have reduced your options for hiring skilled programmers in the labor market. Some system analysts and senior programmer analysts may be quite familiar with several languages and compilers but usually prefer to work with only one, possibly two. Many programmers are experienced in one language and possess only a rough familiarity with capabilities of other compilers. Not all translaters offer identical facilities for meeting and handling user requirements. Some machines and languages are not suitable for commercial data processing. We shall examine and discuss, with limitations, the common compilers and the possible advantages and disadvantages involved in their selection for your needs.

The more common compilers in widespread usage are:

1. RPG-II.
2. COBOL.
3. Assembler.
4. Fortran.

Other specialized languages are available for use in commercial shops, but the above list is intended only to represent the more common compilers. Some installations will be using various combinations including specialized languages developed for specific applications. However, the list is fairly representative of languages used in many small- to medium-sized installations. Each language possesses characteristics eminently suitable for certain designated applications. Likewise, each compiler contains built-in restrictions, making it virtually unusable for all applications. A compiler must produce an effective set of program instructions to satisfy user needs, making good use of hard- and software combinations. This effectiveness will be measured in benefits for the installation and user departments.

RPG-II

The early days of the original RPG were something of a disaster. The inherent weaknesses, which became quickly apparent, and limitations gave the language a bad reputation which lingers to this day. Older, more experienced programmers, who have not kept up with their trade, continue to remember RPG as being suitable only for very limited report-writing processes. The modern RPG-II is a powerful language with enhancements and capabilities, eminently suitable for large commercial applications. Instruction manuals are complete and extensive. This language is easy to learn, and the instructions set provides powerful options. There is sufficient power for many sophisticated business applications.

Use of RPG-II affords benefits not easily measurable in terms of machine efficiency. The structure of any RPG program is virtually self-explanatory in detailed logic flow. This allows an outsider (perhaps an EDP auditor) to examine source statements and follow program flow. Files to be used are clearly identified and labeled. Input specifications are carefully limited to defined files, fields, and records. Arrays and tables are defined in extension specifications. By program definition, calculations can only be performed against items included and made a part of the program structure. It is possible to create new files, fields and records, but not without definition. Access to other files or routines outside the normal cycle may be accomplished through use of program exits written in assembler routines. Program exits may affect data security, but these routines all require careful definition. Output specifications follow a logical pattern allowing quick understanding. The logic flow is reasonable, though restrictive, when measured against other compilers. Calculation requirements translate in a mnemonic fashion for ready comprehension. The enhancement of array processing has done much to extend capabilities of the language, adding new dimensions of computing power for the commercial user. Efficient use of internal subroutines creates internal substructures, making for efficient processing, programming, and debugging.

Popularity of the System 3, and later System 32's helped to create a pool of skilled RPG programmers. These skills may have developed through a comparatively small configuration, but this exposure to electronic capabilities produces experience and competence unrelated to installation size. For the small business, availability of experienced programmers will aid in minimizing staffing problems.

In choosing RPG-II for its many virtues, you cannot overlook the disadvantages. For mathematical calculations, this compiler is not the most effective. Time required for writing and executing mathematical computations in RPG can be almost prohibitive in terms of total performance. Program structure is very confining and not subject to ready alteration. Depending upon the specific program complexities, RPG-II will also consume large amounts of core. As an installation grows and prospects of a larger mainframe are introduced into the planning framework, you should be aware of the shortage of skilled programmers and support for a System 370 using RPG. Based on future needs, this could eliminate RPG from early consideration and simultaneously reduce future prospects for a later language conversion. RPG is similar to any other resource—weigh and evaluate before using. This is very definintely a long-range decision.

Assembler Language

Assembly language is not considered to be a high-level compiler. Very basic instructions reduce man-made instructions to (almost) machine language. There are some prewritten macro routines available, but in many instances, programmers are required to write their own. The use of assembly language will result in significant lowering of core requirements for many applications. Future maintenance requirements for programs written in assembly may be difficult and time-consuming due to different programming styles and/or assumptions. There are occasions when this compiler offers valuable benefits for the small user, but in a small shop, Assembler should not be considered as the prime language.

Fortran

Fortran is a powerful compiler, flexible and efficient for mathematical computations. Commercial versions of Fortran are available, but true suitability may be limited to specific applications. For an engineering application, Fortran may be an absolute necessity. The language is mathematical in nature, lending itself to repetitive computation of data in and through mathematical formulas. In actual practice, Fortran should be used for special purposes in a commercial shop. It is a standard language transportable between machine configurations and vendors.

PL-1

Introduction of PL-1 as a new language represents an attempt to offer a dual-purpose compiler, suitable for commercial use and to meet additional requirements of mathematical and scientific users. Like many another hybrid, there are certain advantages and limitations. The PL-1 compiler offers economies of core usage for mathematical calculations, but will require much additional core in commercial applications. The increasing usage of mathematically derived formulas for commercial processing may make this compiler a powerful tool for extensive use in the development of modeling and simulation programs for commercial applications.

The availability of skilled PL-1 programmers is somewhat limited. Many users with extensive programming and development costs invested in other languages have been reluctant to make a major conversion to PL-1. Standards are not 100% compatible across product lines of all vendors.

COBOL

Development of COBOL may be traced back to an insistence by the Federal government on a compiler independent of any vendor and readily portable across product lines. It is a powerful language, offering extreme flexibility to the user, and is almost self-documenting. Instructions are in English-like terms and are easily read and readily understood. Unlike RPG's restrictive logic, COBOL offers the programmer a free form of software logic. COBOL, widely used for commercial applications, is almost a universal language. In terms of core requirements, COBOL consumes usable core in large quantities, even for simple listings with limited computational needs. There are many versions or sub-sets available in various forms suitable for use on any System 3 with sufficient core.

Compiler Summary

The selection of a compiler, or compilers, is a long-range decision with many implications. Each language offers varying capabilities and advantages. There are inherent limitations in each choice. Personal preference may be a major factor, but long-range considerations should include the possibility of a major compiler conversion as the shop grows in complexity. Small systems frequently begin with RPG, and probably this choice is valid for several years. No compiler choice is irrevocable, and there may come a time when language conversion is mandated. As the small user migrates upwards through product lines from various vendors, RPG tends to lose some popularity to COBOL—especially in the breaking line between small-or-medium and large shops.

The choice is yours; certainly it is not an easy decision. Options are to be explored carefully—the selection of a language for your computer is one involving present and future needs.

Review Questions

1.   Is it a must for managers to have programming skills? Should the manager be the best programmer in the installation?

2.   Describe differences between specifics of programming and the general skills required for management.

3.   What is the situation when a manager orders a change in compilers, and is unskilled in using the new compiler?

4.   List circumstances where RPG-II is not an adequate choice for a compiler. Do the same with Fortran, COBOL, and Assembler.

chapter 13

Employee Selection and Training Considerations

If you have solved the problem of an available labor force, employee selection and training should be your next consideraton. It is not sufficient to follow standard hiring practices of personnel selection through the usual forms of measurement. People with an aptitude for data processing come in all sizes, shapes, and colors. No single test or battery of tests can be used reliably and exclusively in selecting DP personnel. The most important personal trait necessary in an employee is an open, inquiring mind. Self-motivation must be present, but it may be your function to supply additional motivation. The best employees seem to have an aptitude for change and a "quick" mind. Locating personnel with these qualities is, at best, a difficult task. If an applicant meets your requirements, hire this person quickly, before someone else does. Talent combinations may readily be utilized in many problem-solving situations. For an engineering firm, certain mathematical and spatial analysis skills may be an absolute necessity. In the commercial firm, a facility for number manipulation and verbal comprehension may be extremely valuable. The right combination of skills will fit your needs, but there does not seem to be one single answer to the problem of employee selection. You may substitute completed college years as a method for measuring motivation. This may be valid to the extent of counting x number of courses multiplied by semesters. It may measure motivation or determination to complete an assigned task—although occasionally it may prove to be an invalid selection mode.

Some schools and universities place undue emphasis on "school solutions" and too little on innovative techniques used to attack a problem. Your greatest potential for hiring success may be in the person who regards every task as a personal challenge in problem-solving. This challenge may also be directed toward production techniques. Problem-solving processes are adaptable to the techniques of brain-storming. Programmers or analysts with "far out" ideas may also have a "far out" solution to effectively solve problems. Personnel selection, experienced or unskilled, should be based on potential, not past experiences. For example, I have heard of more than one manager informing an applicant—"We hire *on* potential and pay *for* performance."

On-going training is an absolute necessity. Continuing improvements and developments are such that the learning process cannot stop with simple mastery of a language or one machine. New techniques and new hardware combine to make a career in data processing one of continual education. If your shop is to remain in the forefront of data processing, you must stay constantly aware of new developments to ready your staff for the future. The key to success for an installation will be a program designed to continually improve methods and technology. A manager without a budget for additional training is limiting personal professional growth and encouraging stagnation. To paraphrase an advertising slogan—"Training doesn't cost, it pays." In your role, one of your responsibilities is to train the staff to meet changing requirements of enterprise. A well-trained staff, motivated to improve skills and professional competence through training and leadership, will make your job as a manager easier and simpler.

Staffing Availability

A computer is an inanimate object resting quietly in a machine room until there are personnel available to communicate needs and wants to the machine. What talents are required to communicate with a computer? What skills are necessary for staffing a DP installation?

An existing installation has a decided advantage over one soon to be installed. Without formalized job descriptions many data entry operators are aware of the necessary requirements to meet production standards. A computer operator understands the need for producing the payroll on a definite time schedule. A programmer may be concerned about the new financial statements and a proposed revision of a reporting system. The manager is contemplating a decision recommending a major change in configuration. At minimum, a new shop must be considered a venture into the unknown. Before this new experience can be successful, an installation must be competently and adequately staffed. A staff breathes life and spirit into the shop. Before discussing and considering specific problems of staffing, you must consider the basic jobs to be performed within a shop. These basic tasks are:

1. Data entry.
2. Programming.
3. Operations.
4. Management.

These basics will be required in every computer installation. It is your task to understand the interrelation of jobs and tasks as they relate to the corporate organization.

Data Entry Function

Data entry is an inclusive term that ranges from highly specialized talents for the key-punch operator to an airline employee entering flight reservations through a key-driven terminal. Data entry, as a generic term, refers to the centralized office with specialized equipment and staff for handling substantial volumes of input data. This is a valid, though narrow, concept. When all entry devices were key-punches and verifiers, this may have been a reasonable definition. The term key-punch operator has fallen into disuse as additional duties and responsibilities have been added to the job. Locations and titles have changed as new responsibilities and tasks have increased the scope of job duties. Data entry is a process for capturing data and/or information with the aid of an electromechanical device for subsequent use in a different machine. This definition will hold true for the president or chairman of the board and the specialized operator who enters data into any system. The task of data entry clearly crosses job and departmental lines. A reservations clerk may enter data into the computer. The president is performing a similar task by requesting sales reports (from existing data) through a CRT on his desk. The basic assignments will remain—changing over the years with new technological developments—providing for the physical act of posting or entering information into a computer.

If your installation is operating with clearly defined job duties, you will have the task of staffing for data entry. Staffing for this selection is of prime importance in fulfilling managerial responsibilities. This section, be it one person or 250, is a human interface communicating information (from differing sources) into the computer complex. Under certain conditions and circumstances, operators may be empowered to make limited decisions for acceptance or rejection of data. Information, once recorded or captured, may flow through a variable number of computer programs and become a factor in a multi-million dollar decision. Important? Yes, absolutely vital. The data entry department deserves, and should receive, the same amount of careful planning consideration as any other department in your installation.

The Programming Function

Programming is a process instructing the computer to perform definite prescribed operations. Without programs, the machine obviously will not be productive. Computer programming is more than the simple solving of business problems with electronic methods and techniques. It is the application of brain power in solving business-related problems through the judicious application of computer processes. To an outsider, this appears to be a relatively simple function; experience, however, usually proves otherwise. A program can be compared to a fine Swiss watch—performing one function very well. But effective computer programming is more than the performance of one narrowly defined task. It will represent a balance of time, instructions and assumptions, and power of the computer configuration.

A computer, large or small, is only as effective as the programs supplied by a programmer. Resources of a computer are defined within a finite limit. The programming function is a tool, the utilitarian device enabling the machine to perform its assigned duties to and beyond specified limits. There are, however, programs and programmers that stretch the computer to its defined limit of capabilities. The object of computer programs is to provide services and reports beneficial to the corporation. There is a delicate balance between machine utilization and programming efficiency that must be attained. It is common for the urgencies of a business to insist upon production before a program has been adequately tested and documented. This is not good practice and should be discouraged. Programs represent investments of time, money, equipment, and human talent. Effective programs also represent the combined efforts of the staff. Printouts, resulting from effective programming, are a visible record of productive achievement for your department.

Operations

Similar to an assembly line, computer operations represent the coming together of data and programs for assembly and final production. Operational responsibilities include the meeting of production schedules imposed by external influences. There are additional duties involved in balancing reports to insure accuracy, de-leaving carbon paper, and checking a report distribution schedule. The combination of these operational factors is similar to a recipe calling for all ingredients, instructions, pots and pans, and multiple ovens to be used simultaneously. To meet these requirements calls for careful balancing of internal resources and external schedules. It may be necessary to reschedule jobs, delaying high-priority tasks in favor of less important activities. This situation may or may not be indicative of poor scheduling. The seemingly questionable decision for priority production may be very wise. Rescheduling for company efficiency (not just the computer room) will have the desired effect of placing completed processing in the hands of more user departments more rapidly. Long production runs, using large quantities of machine time, may delay several user departments. Like the assembly line, the entire production process must be equitable in providing the greatest good for the greatest number. Scheduling priority has the advantage of multiplying services for all users.

To balance the operations function, the entire process must be judged and carefully evaluated. Priority scheduling also extends into all departments. Relatively small tasks (for key-driven operations) may require inordinate amounts of processing time in relation to data volume. Production activities are assigned the duty and responsibility for meeting reasonable schedules. Computer-generated information provides the user with tangible results representing the combined efforts of your staff.

Review Questions

1. What are the traits you would look for in conducting a search for new employees?

2. "We hire on potential and pay for performance." Is this a valid statement? If not, why not?

3. In staffing an installation, there are four basic functions. Describe each in detail. Which should be rated most important?

4.   The availability of a labor pool provides the opportunity to pick and choose the most desirable employee for each job. Describe how you would use this labor pool if you were faced with the need for training new employees for each major job function.

chapter 14

Extracurricular Duties
for the Manager

With appointment as manager come the ancillary duties not covered or included in formal job descriptions. A portion of these duties must be devoted to membership and active participation in selected trade and professional organizations. The value of membership in a specific group may be debatable, but participation in one or more associations is fulfilling, leading to greater knowledge and understanding of the industry and your chosen profession. There are several groups offering many benefits for the systems user. If there is an option for participation, you must choose a group or chapter offering the most benefits. It would be worthwhile to consider a local civic club or organization. In most instances the club will welcome your active participation, but such activities, though personally rewarding, do little to improve your position as a manager. Professional organizations and trade groups offer the quickest means of realizing a corporate dividend on time and efforts. The trade and professional associations are there to evaluate, discuss, and propose solutions for various common problems. Specialized groups also offer the opportunity of rubbing shoulders (and bending elbows) with peer groups. Many data processing associations offer important benefits for the professional in DP.

To name only a few associations achieving professional reputations for excellence is to omit the names of other fine groups. As a matter of practice, most national groups cater to needs of the larger installation, not those of the small-to-medium shop. There is a language barrier and lack of a common ground for understanding. Problems may be almost identical, but small users are not accorded equal consideration. The general feeling may be compared to that of flying a Piper Cub to a convention of Boeing 747's. Both perform the same job, but in a widely divergent context. Within the associations there may exist special interest groups. This select group may offer valuable services. In considering membership in a

national, or local, group, bear in mind: You will only get out of the group what you put into it. It is insufficient to purchase membership; you must make contributions to the group. Participation is the name of the game, paying off in professional stature and advancing your personal position. Some of the national groups are listed below:

1. Data Processing Management Association
    505 Busse Highway
    Park Ridge, Illinois 60068
2. American Federation of Information Processing Societies
3. Association for Systems Management
4. Association for Computing Machinery
5. Local System 3 Group's

Membership in any or all groups may be desirable, depending upon your desire for participation and advancement in data processing.

An association will have individual chapters located in many urban centers. Before making a commitment of time and money for participation in any group, go as a visitor to observe the proceedings. Though purposes of a national organization are worthwhile, you may find the local chapter to be weak and ineffective. Leadership required for the strength of a local group may be strong, inbred, or nonexistent. Frequently the local club or group which is nationally unaffiliated may have strong leaders interested in advancing the cause of data processing with religious zeal. Before you opt for membership and active participation, be sure the club or chapter will meet your needs and expectations.

Within various industry groups—insurance, supermarkets, banking, credit associations, etc.—are specific subcommittees researching, meeting, and discussing common fields of interest. These specialized associations will have subgroups for auditing, advertising, and data processing, etc. Regardless of size, these specialized meetings offer concentrated discussions of universal industry problems as they relate to DP. For example, open discussions and debates concerning scanning systems for the retail industry and suermarket systems would have been impossible without active participation from interested vendors and potential users represented in each subcommittee. On the other hand, if you are employed by an oil and gas producer, sessions concerning EFT (electronic funds transfer) may be of little immediate value or interest.

Industry trade groups offer similar trade problems and a commonality of solutions. The advantages are not so much realized in specific ideas and approaches, but in a compounding of viewpoints from the multiple resources of peer groups. You may attend a seminar for general data processing and learn of new techniques suitable for large installations which may be quickly adapted for specific use in any type of enterprise. Usable solutions involving data and computer room security will be very beneficial regardless of source or industry. Magnitudes of the problem may change, but basic theories remain the same. Go—and learn. Seminars may offer a "shotgun" approach, but if you can bring one worthwhile idea or innovation back to your installation, the expenses are well justified.

A role in professional organizations will also serve the educational purpose of maintaining a constant flow of information concerning recent advances in the field. This type of association can serve you by affording opportunities for learning based on experiences of others, helping you to avoid the same mistakes. You may have to discard much of the information, but you are building a fund of knowledge and possible solutions for future problems.

Maintain Relations with Other Installations

To provide for unexpected contingencies, you should establish and maintain a good working relationship with other installations similar to yours. There is always the distinct possibility of machine failure occurring just as the payroll is being written, or alternatively of fire or flood delaying production. Other installations probably may not have the same exact configuration, but at least you may be able to borrow time or buy some machine hours in case of a real emergency.

In addition to the backup provisions, other installations may provide machine time for those applications requiring more computing power than your equipment has on call at the time. Other installation managers, time permitting, are usually willing to cooperate with outsiders on a personal, informal basis. This is not to suggest your backup or short-term emergency situation provisions are to be made with a competitive firm.

If a working relationship is too friendly and cooperative between competing firms, the FTC (Federal Trade Commission) may regard this to be conspiracy against others, prompting restraint of trade injunctions, etc. This situation also admits to the possibility of corporate information and practices being inadvertently disclosed between arch rivals.[1] It is possible

---

[1]In my own installation, we have maintained a working relationship with competitive firms, but there has been no sharing of confidential matters. As a matter of fact, the two installations will admit only that payroll is an existing application, with no discussions of methodology for meeting schedules, etc.

to limit your contact to only pure technical problems and the sharing of information only as it relates to DP with no industry references.

If you do have friends and acquaintances in the industry, this will allow contact for informal salary surveys, and the easy verification of past work experiences is also possible when reviewing an application from a prospective employee. Other installations also provide sources of information concerning new techniques and developments. Even if you maintain subscriptions and do active research, some opportunities will be missed unless another manager discusses these items with you. The informal grapevine runs through the trade just as it floats through the internal organizations. Without the formalities of trade groups or clubs, there are managers who are quite willing to visit, by phone or in person, and discuss common problems and topics of general interest. These sessions may be highly productive in terms of benefits realized.

Public Speaking

Some individuals regard speaking in public as worse than ordeal by fire. This reaction is perhaps normal to the inexperienced. In considering all factors, the opportunity for public speaking to various groups is a chance to improve your skills for management presentations. Most civic and trade organizations inviting an after-dinner speaker recognize a need for additional communication with the outside world. If you are reluctant to portray yourself as an expert, just remember your company has chosen you to be the resident expert in data processing. Outside speaking engagements may include high school, college, or special interest groups.

A high school group or groups of classes offer the greatest challenge and simultaneously may be the easiest audience. A younger audience will not accept generalized statements without a reasonable amount of supporting facts. At the same time, their experiences may be so limited as to exclude difficult questions that you may be reluctant to answer. This experience affords you the occasion to improve your organization for presentations, and the experience to speak extemporaneously. There are other personal dividends. By sharing your experiences with younger members of society, you are making friends and encouraging those who are interested to come into the world of DP. There are many people presently employed in the industry because someone made an interesting presentation concerning the excitement and benefits to be experienced while working in data processing. After high school and college students come the professional groups unrelated to data processing.

With a diverse group of individuals who may never see a computer, but are interested, you have the chance to improve your professional standing as a manager. To foster understanding and comprehension in groups of this nature will require a strict avoidance of technical terms and excellent interpretation of DP problems and opportunities. In some meetings you may be asked to justify the threat of automation, or discuss the frightening possibilities of 1984 as they relate to computer application in modern society. These are to be regarded as opportunities for enhancing the profession and your standing in the data processing community. DP is not an arcane science.

Professional Publications and Journals

In a young, exciting industry, there is a veritable flood of technical and trade journals discussing at length the most miniscule details. Data processing is no exception. There are publications ranging from the most erudite of papers down to and including the lowest of "How I won the Irish Sweepstakes through the use of an esoteric subroutine branching through 29 other complicated routines." Some publications offer more benefits to the small user. Others are so far ahead, technologically, of the small system users as to be difficult to read and understand. There is value in almost all of them, though it is not always easy to separate valuable articles from those inapplicable to specific tasks and applications—but, no one ever really believed that working in data processing was going to be easy. Trade journals, difficult to understand though they may be, do offer intriguing hints and suggestions as to future directions for the industry. In the book *Data Processing, 1959 Proceedings*,[2] there is a discussion by General Leslie R. Groves, U.S. Army (retired) and then vice president of the Remington Rand Division, Sperry Rand Corporation, on the management of time and selling upward. This same volume contains a limited discussion of centralized data processing.[3] Even the venerable Dr. Grace Murray Hopper discusses compiler development subsequent to the A-2 Compiler which was used for mathematical and scientific problems in 1953. These topics have not been concluded yet. Many of the current journals continue to include news articles and papers concerning these subjects. There may not be one answer, but certainly these subjects have

[2] *Data Processing 1959*, Charles H. Johnson, Editor, National Machines Accountants Association, Mt. Prospect, Ill., pp. 15–19.

[3] Ibid., pp. 109–112.

been thoroughly discussed in the most minute detail for any installation manager. Other topics include continuing papers on compilers, effective programming, the continuing functional enlargement of the mini-computer, data base techniques, and communications processing. All are valuable to some degree. The problems facing a manager are to stay current in the field and yet not spend every waking minute perusing technical journals.

The list of publications below includes those distinguished for their immediate interest and the quality of their articles. Some offer specific benefits—such as *Infosystems*, which tends to concentrate on communications processing. Others are more general, offering topics of wider interest. The following list is both eclectic and pragmatic:

1. *Datamation*
2. *Small Systems World*
3. *Infosystems*
4. *Computer Decisions*
5. *Computerworld*

Computerworld is a weekly newspaper serving informational needs of the DP community and does not quite fit in with other publications of a periodic nature. It is the quickest means of following the industry on a news basis. The monthly trade magazines are less concerned with immediate external forces surrounding DP, but are more concerned with technical and philosophical discussions.

Small Systems World, published by Informatics Inc., is a comparatively young publication. Devoted to the small system user, this monthly brings a compendium of user-written articles, new product announcements, and occasional features dealing with specific techniques or hardware comparisons. Editorial comment is at a minimum. As the System 3 has increased with powerful increments and additions, so has the number of articles concerning data base, MRP, IPICS, and other exotics for the small user.

This magazine, for the young beginning manager, brings short, concise articles concerning topics of immediate interest and potential use. The content and level of each paper has increased slowly and surely since the original issue in 1972, reflecting the increased sophistication in "little" shops. There is limited mention of non-IBM, small computer systems. The magazine has included these in the section devoted to new announcements and will print subsequent articles reflecting degrees of success as the equipment develops. There is a not unreasonable amount of space reserved for problem-solving techniques, complete with flowcharts and program instructions.

With its primary emphasis on the concept of distributed processing, *Computer Decisions* is a valuable addition to your suggested reading list. Each month attention is focused on distributed processing techniques and planning methods. Additional features cover a wide spectrum of interests including nontechnical articles of general interest. As with many of the others, this publication includes new products, software offerings, general news and industry observations, and technical announcements which may be of specific interest. *Computer Decisions* is a particularly easy to read and understand periodical.

As the official publication of the Data Processing Management Association, *Data Management* has much space devoted to various member activities and achievements. The articles are usually directed toward the commercial user. A typical month may include a learned discussion of software measurement methods and evaluation, proposals for developing professional standards in an installation, and suggestions for managing time or management by objectives. There is space reserved for national topics and legislative interests. Like many other publications, there are the usual pages for news items of interest.

Relatively small amounts of attention and space are reserved for the small user. This is perhaps a reflection of the membership, but does not detract from the usefulness of topics of general management interest found valuable for any size of installation.

Datamation is one of the largest and most successful of the publications devoted exclusively to data processing. There are the usual departments and excellent columns and comments submitted by staff and readers. Articles and papers are of high quality with occasional lapses into humor which are eminently readable and amusing. The topics cover a wide range of subject matter and user interest. For specialized topics (such as EFT), there are in-depth discussions providing a complete summary of pros and cons, and/or a running commentary on subjects of national interest. *Datamation* devotes issues to one major topic, such as software management or computer architectures. For the small systems manager, this publication offers continuing coverage of the industry's progress—in large systems, small systems, and other variations—with particular attention being devoted to topics for future use in shops of any magnitude.

In building a reading list for improvement of management skills, care must be taken to insure quality and not quantity. Your reading or study time as a manager will be limited to brief time spans at the office and most likely, a sizable pile of journals to read at home or on the commuter train. Pick your sources wisely and use them to their fullest. Similar to a seminar, publications and journals offer many thought-provoking ideas, any one of which may be a valuable tool in improving operational skills and enhancing your management techniques.

Review Questions

1. Do professional DP groups have sufficient value from membership to warrant your participation?

2. Reading and perusing of trade journals is a time-consuming task. Does this maintenance of industry awareness offer benefits sufficient to warrant the required time for reading?

chapter 15

Internal
Departmental Relations

In considering the advantages for growth and advancement through public speaking, talks, or seminars, do not overlook the real benefits of sharing information with employees from within your organization. If your shop is providing services for the corporation, worthwhile progress may be made by conducting tours—short, brief, and informative. For those with a greater need to know, you may wish to conduct a few sessions of an introductory nature presenting humorous horror stories of what went wrong and showing how information passes through many steps to insure accuracy. Educational seminars such as these should be informally structured, ungraded, and be related to specific topics for ready understanding and comprehension. In all circumstances, take every necessary step to ensure complete absence of technical jargon.

Perhaps the easiest example to use is the simple personnel roster. Everyone has a name and will comprehend the statistics associated with a personnel roster. They may lack true understanding of the necessity for a roster with detailed uses, but they will relate to the information. In explaining the computer's "black magic box," you may refer to familiar pieces of gear as a reader, brains, and printer, and mention the various filing cabinets or storage devices. Using personnel information, it is fairly easy to lay out and define input specifications for an RPG program. Using the same field names, simply defined of course, it becomes a natural lead-in to define most output requirements. This omits the calculations, but is a natural process for defining and describing steps necessary to write comprehensive calculation instructions. Many employees are aware of the EEOC (Equal Employment Opportunity Commission), but may be unaware of reporting requirements. To relate the problems of incoming data and necessity for tight programming, you may use simple instructions necessary to build field totals for accumulating the total number of employees, number of female employees, and number of men. It is not sufficient to accumulate the total of employees and assume that the total number of employees less the total number of males will equal the number of females. There is the added danger of bad input data, requiring much tighter controls. For example, if your system is using an "M" for males and a "W" for females, this does not allow for the possibility of miscoded information. For statistical accuracy, your instructions and example should include steps necessary to accumulate total number of men, women, and a total number of employees in three separate instructions. Then you use this opportunity to expound on discrepancies in input coding errors. Sessions similar to the one we have described should be short, concise, and *all questions must be answered*. Failure to answer a question will harm your credibility.

If the circumstances will allow, encourage a department head or supervisor, or a lead operator for a department, to go through the process of writing a simple program for a needed project. This operation may use an inordinate amount of your time, but will serve to indoctrinate users with the concept of an effective program to meet project requirements. In selecting this option, use much discretion in choosing a project that is meaningful and requiring only a limited amount of programming skills. This process works well for some instances, so choose your program and the programmer pupil very carefully.

Managerial Duties Summarized

By accepting a job as manager, you have removed yourself from the rank-and-file. With your new-found responsibilities come additional duties above and beyond the traditional eight-to-five job. Many of these duties are unrelated to the job and will require substantial amounts of time (away from the TV tube) devoted to perusing of trade journals and attendance at selected meetings of professional societies and associations. This participation is not a job requirement necessarily, but in attending you are representing your company and enhancing your professional reputation.

Speaking before a group of strangers is not much more difficult than addressing a group of your peers—it only seems to be much more painful. If you have something to say, there will be an audience willing to listen. Your techniques should be polished over a period of time. You have a message to convey. The experiences gained in speaking to an audience will serve well in assembling management presentations for equipment or new applications.

The reading of trade journals is an absolute necessity in maintaining an aura of technical competence and in staying abreast of continuing developments. You should not attempt to have your name placed on every available subscription list. Pick only those publications that will meet your needs. The others, though possibly interesting to read, may not contribute to your situation. It is not necessary to save every issue on the off-chance that you will need to come back and refer to them. Your purposes might be better served by clipping and saving those articles offering new thoughts or approaches of benefit in the future.

As a manager, there are many techniques to be used for accomplishing your job—at work and away from the office. The use of many approaches to advance your position, in and out of the company, will serve to add to your arsenal of managerial skills. Managing or supervising is not an easy job. Becoming a successful manager is more of a career than it appears to the casual onlooker. You must utilize your time and talents to justify the faith that management has placed on you, if you are to fill the shoes of a manager.

Establishing the Integrity of Data Processing

The substitution of a machine to perform tasks heretofore performed by a live person is considered by some as contributing to unemployment, tooth decay, pollution of the environment, and other ills of civilization. It may be likened to a fear of the unknown. There are elements of temporary job displacement, and there will be rumors, much gossip, and possibly even sabotage—deliberate or accidental—when a computer is installed to perform certain tasks. Fears of permanent unemployment are groundless. In fact, the substitution of machines—electronic or mechanical—has done much to raise the standard of living. A machine can perform certain repetitive duties faster and more effectively than most human beings. In addition, mechanical devices do not bear the increasing and costly burden of fringe benefits. Charges for long-distance telephone calls have decreased remarkably with introduction of automatic switching gear and electronic equipment designed to handle growing needs for telephonic communications. Just try to picture a few automatic features removed from your personal life. Your car would not have an automatic transmission, nor a battery-powered self-starter. Tall buildings would not be feasible without elevators. Houses might be illuminated by lanterns or hand-made candles. The list goes on. Every one of these examples was introduced, slowly earned acceptance and gradually became almost a necessity in everyday life.

The same is true of computers. The EDP installation in your company must earn acceptance before company computer usage will become a way of corporate life. There are two possibilities that might befall the new installation: (1) total failure; and (2) slow progress toward acceptance. For our purposes, we shall consider the process of acceptance as one of many steps necessary to establish the integrity of the DP department. Your machine will be performing thousands, possibly millions of computer instructions on a daily basis. These machine commands are represented in the form of programs—written by fallible human beings. Somewhere in these operations exists a potential for error. It is your task to minimize errors and earn respect from the user departments. Reliability of the entire DP installation can be achieved through your efforts. We shall be mentioning and discussing some major areas to be aware of in building a professional installation with high standards required for satisfactory performance.

Accuracy-in

A new shop is faced with the problem and opportunity of introducing computer discipline. Computer discipline is the establishment of external and internal standards necessary for the satisfactory application of computer logic to the processing of data. Like computer standards for programming, there must be guidelines and rules for the data to be processed. The accountants have used a "trial balance" as a kind of guideline for many years. The addition of electronic power has imposed more stringent requirements for all data to be processed. Guidelines establish standards by their existence. The procedures for utilizing existing assumptions will be of much value in establishing internal professional standards and integrity. If an organization is relatively small and unsophisticated, you may be required to cross departmental lines to make recommendations and suggestions for ensuring the accuracy of data for processing. User departments may not be so willing to accept recommendations from an outsider. Suggestions from an outsider may be rejected out-of-hand, or they may be accepted grudgingly as an unnecessary rule. Individual department heads may consider suggestions from someone outside the department as criticism and an infringement of responsibilities. There are elements of truth in this assumption. If you are willing to accept responsibility for the accuracy of your work processed through the computer, then it becomes the responsibility of other department supervisors to ensure the efficacy of work performed under their direction.

Establishing the accuracy and discipline of externally supplied computer input is a joint responsibility for you and user departments. For your first venture into other departments, you would be wise not to insist upon highly sophisticated standards. Work and consult with department heads. They are quite aware of their internal problems and can make helpful suggestions for incorporation of necessary controls. If other departments are willing to work with you, the standards become a joint responsibility—painless to install and simple to implement. It may take a period of time to earn cooperation from other departments and supervisors. However, like Rome, you will not implement nor achieve all goals in one day. The process is slow, but necessary. The implications of accuracy required for data coming in for processing also carry the strictest assumption of accuracy in computer-generated output. This responsibility is solely yours and is not shared with other departments.

Accuracy-out

Everyone assumes that processed work coming from the computer is error-free. Supposedly, computers never make mistakes, and this report came from the computer, etc. The frequency of actual computer errors is rare. The chances for mistakes as a result of programming inaccuracies are much greater. Incorrect data submitted to and processed undetected through a process of computer-generated checks and balances is still wrong, but responsibility for the fault may be placed on your shoulders. Correct establishment of guidelines for accuracy-in will tend to eliminate flaws of this type. Guidelines for accuracy are also referred to as controls. Your responsibilities are to use all available methods and techniques to minimize undetected errors.

The power of the computer may be applied to various edits and audits to ensure validity before data is released for processing. Perhaps the simplest control is a predetermined total tape with or without document count. If a process is for general ledger accounting, a simple edit may be made an internal operation of the job stream. This edit might check the apparent validity of account numbers, store or location numbers, and other selected items. This edit does not replace controls from the user department; it adds needed strength to the complete procedure. Edits of this nature are not meant to be a reflection on the user department. It actually strengthens your role if you have managed to "flag" an error condition that should not be allowed entry into the system. The substitution of electronics for human effort will reduce and/or eliminate careless errors causing expensive reruns.

If there is a genuine error in computer-supplied information, you are faced with two responsibilities. First, if it is a flaw directly traceable to activities within your department, you must gracefully accept total responsibility for the error. Your second duty is to analyze the situation and take effective steps to prevent recurrence of this problem. Your integrity as a manager will be damaged if you attempt to shift blame to one of your employees, or if you excuse the mistake as a computer error. User departments will doubt your credibility if you are unwilling to shoulder responsibility for your errors. Staff members under your control and guidance will lose respect if you fault them to user departments. Data processing is your total responsibility and cannot be delegated, nor shifted to a staff member.

Managing Accuracy

The problems of accuracy are jointly shared with user departments. The implementation of standards for accuracy may be almost totally in your hands as DP manager. Verification processes lose their effectiveness when certain steps and procedures are skipped or overlooked. This may result in errors untraceable to flaws in technique. If external methods are deemed adequate, your internal procedures should never be omitted. Responsibility for accuracy is vested in DP, and it is your duty to maintain acceptable standards. Sloppy or careless processing will destroy effectiveness of any monitoring procedure. User department errors may tend to create problems by calling for management intervention. This should be accomplished at departmental level, never with the subordinates.

Under some circumstances, user departments may get careless, and the flow of mistakes into the control process may increase beyond what is acceptable. This situation may cause significant decreases in production efficiency. If an operator is trying to be helpful, work may be returned to the user department employee for correction. If allowed to continue, the situation will deteriorate to a point where DP is processing increasing numbers of edits or balances caused by careless preparation of input. Employees in user departments get careless at their jobs, relying on the computer and operator to keep them out of trouble. It is not good for this condition to develop.

If an operator continues to confer directly with other departmental employees, you are losing control of the situation. An operator's responsibility does not consist of interdepartmental liaison. While an operator is away from the computer, it may be idle; thus costing valuable production time. The operator is losing personal productivity while in the user department. This is to say nothing of lost time in the other department. Situations similar to this may remain undetected for months until the lost time factor becomes noticeable. It is never too late for corrective action, but remedial steps should have been taken long before degeneration became so apparent.

In the situation described above, there are various alternatives for the manager. A choice must be made, and corrective action must be taken. You can abdicate your responsibility as a manager and ignore the problem. In so doing, you will be faced with a slow degeneration of the operation. Your solution must involve the other department head. It may be impossible for a supervisor to be aware of every operation performed by an employee each day. However, if employees from another department are inhibiting progress of your work, then it becomes your personal duty to bring this to attention of the employees' supervisor. If you take corrective steps, circumventing the other supervisor, you are giving that supervisor the right to bypass your authority and go directly to employees in your department. This destroys control and dilutes authority. The simple process of a visit to a user department with reasonable questions about edits and processes will work wonders for improving the quality of input.

No supervisor enjoys the prospect of another department head questioning the efficiency and effectiveness of a subordinate. Supervisor-to-supervisor confrontations get questions resolved without finger-pointing by the guilty parties. This is a two-way street—other department heads should be asked, and instructed, to bring potential computer problems and complaints to your attention, not to one of your employees. This principle is basic for maintaining chain of command with line and staff relationships.

Moreover, bypassing of authority may be symptomatic of problems not yet surfaced. Few employees are quick to admit errors, shortcomings, and failures. The symptoms of bypassing authority may indicate unreasonable checkpoints or a reluctance to bear responsibility (and pride) for work accomplishments or failures. Some situations similar to the ones described previously may indicate employees trying to win a personal popularity contest. Any department head is charged with a responsibility that rises above personalities and individuals. For you to succeed in your position, you must be sure your staff is carrying its weight, and not the burden of other departments. This is not meant to convey feelings of heartlessness. What you should be concerned about is your position. Anyone not contributing to the fulfillment of your assignment may be working against you. The entire situation is more complex than is indicated. There are circumstances, excuses, and reasons which may have an ameliorating effect upon your decisions. There may be an immediate solution for the problem. However, positive action, promptly taken, will have the needed effect of diminishing the problem. It will take time to solve some problems. In the meantime, you may be required to work around them.

The question of internal errors is quite different, though related to problems in user departments. Internal questions may emerge as a result of erroneous programming assumptions, changing situations, or company growth problems. Regardless of the stated reason, responsibility is fairly well fixed inside the department. Programming errors are frequently based on invalid assumptions. This will afford the opportunity of examining a program or procedure against performance and stated expectations. Eruption of an error indicates a potential problem. If one problem exists, there is a distinct possibility of other similar difficulties. The mistake may be symptomatic of a complete series of wrong assumptions programmed into the operation. (At one phase in my career, I discovered an operator making program changes to accommodate a user department. These changes were against all policy. The operator is no longer with us.) The problems of managing an installation in a rapidly changing environment present unique problems and challenges for the supervisor.

All too frequently the company will make decisions without informing the computer room manager. This may arise when a company is in a period of rapid expansion or operating departments are in a state of change and reorganization. Most installations seem to be in a constant state of change. It would also appear that needs for information are changing with increasing frequency. Computer response time may be measured in milliseconds, and minor programming changes are seemingly easy to implement. The adaptability tends to create an aura of false security inside user departments. Other internal operations may tend to overlook submitting new additional changes until the last instant. Without notification of change, there is no logical reason for holding any division accountable for errors of omission. Unhappily, this is frequently the case for the machine room.

Without complete, reliable information, your computer is, or will be, burdened with rushed program patches on an emergency basis. By definition of duties, it becomes a responsibility for an originating department to supply all needed data in a timely fashion. Information may be supplied from several sources. You may ensure this flow of information by maintaining good relations with other departments. With little necessity for creating a furor, you can impress every department with the need for accurate information prior to processing.

Relative ease of program modification tends to lull the users into a false sense of security. Some changes are quickly inserted into programs, and production, in a few minutes. Other changes, apparently similar in nature, may require several hours or days to implement. This seeming paradox is difficult to explain to all users. If you do try to explain the differences in time, do so in simple, nontechnical terms and avoid jargon where possible. A retreat into jargon implies the listener cannot comprehend your problem in plain English. For some audiences, moderate use of technical terms may increase their level of understanding.

Insisting upon a reasonable advance notice for programming and testing of changes should allow adequate lead time for responding to reasonable requests. Program modification may be a maintenance function without schedules, implying a certain amount of crash priorities. There are various ways to minimize the problem and reduce it to a manageable task. One such device is a program change request.

Program Change Requests

A program change request form (later referred to as PCR) will serve many purposes. The PCR illustrated in Figure 5 is a sample form designed to meet needs for one company. Inclusion of this sample does

PLEASE CHECK BOX
NEW PROGRAM REQUEST
PROGRAM CHANGE REQUEST
PROGRAM CHANGE NOTIFICATION

Figure 5: Program Change Request

REQUESTED BY _____ DATE _____
REASON FOR CHANGE _____
DESCRIPTION OF CHANGE_____

AUTHORIZED BY _____ DATE_____
PROGRAM NAME _____PROGRAM NUMBER_____
ESTIMATED PROGRAMMING TIME _____
ESTIMATED IMPLEMENTATION TIME _____

PROGRAMMER_____ TOTAL TIME_____
START DATE _____
DOCUMENTATION COMPLETE ☐ INITIAL _____
D.P. APPROVAL _____ DATE _____

not imply adequacy in serving the needs of every organization. The form provides for three types of common program changes. It is a responsibility of the user department to specify *in detail* all requirements for a new program. Frequently it may require the combined talents of several department heads in specifying exact requirements. A program change request is a request and/or notification of a necessary modification to an existing program. The notification of program changes would be used when introducing a new form requiring spacing changes, or notice of an impending change of internal factors within a program. Adoption of a similar form will reduce the number of requests for changes. The added benefits (of user-defined specifications) for programming will increase as the user learns how to specify requirements in detail. Involvement in writing specifications frequently requires participation of a member of the programming staff. Other specifications will be considered in following paragraphs.

One of the prime benefits to be derived from a PCR is discipline. Asking for specified requirements may be a nuisance at times, but the nuisance value will be offset by an increase in understanding. Usage of a request form will eliminate the necessity for remembering hurried conversations concerning proposed new changes. Write it—don't say it. Too many programs have been written and rewritten due to faulty instructions at the beginning. Using a PCR form will reduce or eliminate misunderstandings created by a faulty memory.

This PCR contains features which may be of value in many shops. Inclusion of a space for authorizing the change provides discipline and control over priority and project assignment. Without approval, no programming changes are to be made. Also, there are spaces for name of programmer, time estimates, program name/number, etc. Freely adapted for individual needs, any PCR will provide a manager with a reasonable amount of control over job requests, programmer assignments, documentation, and comparisons of actual and estimated times. At the end of a calendar or fiscal year, completed PCR's may be used to review DP progress over the foregoing year. A side benefit worthy of mention: Use the PCR for salary or personal progress reviews. As a project is completed, you may use the back side to record work currently in process or add notations concerning additional program modifications required during the project.

Wisely used, a PCR enables management to maintain internal control over any installation. The discipline gained from this type of internal control is highly valuable. However, do not let the form become a cheap substitute for management involvement. It remains one of your obligations to maintain good working relationships with all personnel utilizing computer services. Users will come to recognize the PCR as a valuable tool for jotting notes and plans to be discussed in future planning sessions if you insist upon its usage and *follow-through*. It is discourteous for the customer (user) to submit a PCR and never receive an acknowledgment. This form may thus serve as a device to improve relations with your customers. It is not a substitute for good management practices, but it can aid in the alleviation of misunderstandings.

Installation Documentation

The entire DP industry is in agreement concerning the importance of documentation. Some of this concern may only be lip service but indicates a genuine concern for what should be considered adequate documentation. Documentation comes in many forms and shapes, all designed to fit a particular need in an existing situation. Along with the evolution of stored-program computers has come a secondary revolution in documentation.

Past Documentation. Realizing that it was difficult, if not impossible, to transfer an adequate picture of a wired accounting machine panel without drafting skills, the early practitioners of DP management began to use a curious form of abbreviation. Very tricky wiring practices were reduced to diagrams for (only) the most complicated portions of a panel. The assumption of user knowledge for the rest of the panel wiring was reasonably valid. The idiosyncracies of electromechanical equipment created more suspicion with the end-user when the "approved" wiring diagram did not always work. As the complexity of early machine processing increased with increasingly lengthy procedures and processes, many managers adopted the practice of flowcharting. The symbols were few, clearly labelled on a template, and clearly indicated the path for a reasonable flow of data. This early documentation was adequate for some shops; but not in all.

As the staff increased, and newcomers were trained to become tabulating machine operators, it became necessary to add words, sentences, and even paragraphs to describe the physical actions to be taken in the passing of cards from one piece of equipment to another. This led to a divided page form of documentation; one half of the page devoted to narrative instructions and descriptions, the other being a flow of charting symbols in sequence with the accompanying paragraphs.

Detailed Flowcharts. With the development of the stored programming concept, simple symbols and verbiage were replaced by larger sheets of paper, new symbols were added, and explanatory words were frequently forced inside the symbols. The shortage of competent experienced programmers, coupled with the then strict forms of programming, created a very lengthy and detailed flowchart. This had the desired effect of documenting program logic. As the flow of programs into daily production increased, so did the paperwork required to keep "adequate" documentation. The sheer volume of changes and additions to existing programs soon made this practice too cumbersome and unwieldy for daily use.

If we examine closely these detailed "Blueprints," we see them as an aid or device, designed to aid the programmer in following logic flow and document assumptions in data flow. In this respect, the detailed flowcharts are invaluable for examining logic. Older, more experienced programmers continue to use bits and pieces of this procedure to picture better the intricacies of some procedures within a program.

Compiler Documentation. Available compilers (and operating systems) now include a built-in form of documentation. For example, the presence of an asterisk in position seven of an RPG record indicates the record is reserved for programmer's comments, and excluded from the program. In COBOL and Fortran, comments are usually indicated in the body of the program.

The competent programmer will use "comment" cards as an easy means of documenting or labelling various field names, indicators, and subroutines. The more experienced programmer will also insert a dated comment into each modificication. This has the additional advantage of time-stamping a change and naming the modification and author. Internal documentation of a program through the use of comment cards is not the final answer/solution to reasonable documentation. It requires a disciplined programmer to follow this practice in keeping internal documentation current.

Reasonable Documentation. Just how much documentation is absolutely required? When the many forms of documentation are considered, it is perhaps even more difficult to decide the needed quantity. It is more or less like asking "How long is a piece of string?" The many items to be included in your checklist would include:

1. Program documentation.
2. Disk layouts.
3. Record layouts.
4. Field codes.
5. Record identification codes.

6. Table and Array definitions.
7. External code structures.
8. Anything that will assist you in managing change.

The conclusion of these items, and others deemed necessary, will bring together the many bits and pieces of data necessary to make changes. Without this disciplined form, it becomes very difficult to make modifications to existing programs. Reference to any item on the checklist has the desired effect of refreshing memory and reinforcing the validity of program assumptions.

In avoiding discussion of the many types of documentation, we should first consider a goal for the installation standard. A workable standard is: A new employee (experienced) should be able to refer to the documentation and continue to operate or manage the shop successfully without detailed and lengthy training. This does not imply the new employee will be instantly efficient in maintaining a smooth well-run operation. It does suggest continuing operation for the computer room, regardless of new personnel. There could be mistakes and false starts, but the operation should continue to function. That is adequate documentation.

Documentation Summary. For some managers, the lack of documentation represents a very shaky form of job security. This concept has caused the demise of many incapable managers. When faced with an emergency, the lack of adequate installation support in the form of runbooks, layouts, and so on, could effectively contribute to the demise of an installation.

There is positive justification for maintaining all supporting books and records. Mere presence of the neatly footnoted runbooks, distribution instructions, etc., give strong indication of competent management. This attention to detail will go far in satisfying the needs of the auditors—internal or external.

One measure of quality management is to be found in the ongoing, operations while the manager is sick or on vacation. The well-run installation will continue to function as well (or better) when the manager is absent. If the shop can function efficiently and well (without the manager's presence), the shop can be said to have adequate documentation.

One comment in the form of a question: If your management wanted to promote you to a much better job, how long would it take you to turn your job over to a successor? If the installation is in good shape, it should be a formality. Otherwise, this promotion could be lost while you are bogged down in the detail of imparting knowledge to your replacement. Think about it.

Outside Consultants

There is a place for outside consultants in your managerial world. The consultant is, or should be, an expert with know-how to assist in problem-solving. With a wide range of experiences and knowledge, the visiting expert can bring many facets of a problem into sharp focus. The role of a counselor should be to observe, advise, and make constructive suggestions. This advisor cannot be expected to substitute in the role of the manager. The manager's role should be enhanced through thoughtful application of a consultant's recommendations. A consultant offers the benefits of:

1.   Prior experience and knowledge.
2.   Unbiased judgment of known factors.
3.   Observation and interviewing skills.

Under no circumstances can the responsibility for decision-making be delegated to a surrogate. An outsider is not expected to be familiar with the inner workings of your installation; only you can be aware of detailed requirements. The consultant can, however, bring to bear benefits from a wide range of experiences. This knowledge is an asset to be carefully applied to the solution of present and future problems. Use this asset— don't let it go to waste.

Presence of an advisor may indicate concern of top management for an existing situation or may be an indication of plans for future needs and an increasing role for data processing. For either reason, be assured that this will afford various opportunities to improve your situation.

On the negative assumption that your shop may be in some un- defined trouble, you have the opportunity to enlist resources from a calm, unbiased mentor in the solution of internal problems you have been un- able to resolve. You can pump, quiz, or otherwise pick the brains of this expert. The flow of information should be two-way; it is to your advantage to be sure it does indeed flow both ways. If this flow of information can be started, you stand to be the beneficiary. Ask questions. Ask for proposed solutions to specific problems. Advice has been said to be worth what it costs. In the case of a consultant, the cost is not inexpensive, and you should utilize this opportunity to gather information of value to you as a manager. For many situations, a visit from the consultant can be turned to profitable use.

If your organization is contemplating a new venture, the consul- tant may be present to advise of possible pitfalls. You have the opportun- ity to explore various options in theory and conversation without costly experimentation. A consulting firm justifies its existence with a continuing flow of successful advice and strongly worded suggestions. The advisor is usually assigned the task of making recommendations; it becomes a matter for the corporate staff to implement these changes, if accepted. As you can imagine, it is relatively simple for the outside expert to make recommendations and not be charged with the responsibility for implementation. The managerial challenge comes through the nuts-and-bolts installation of suggested changes. After these changes, the consultant may be asked to return for further evaluation, thus continuing the cycle.

The client–consultant relationships may be likened to a pyramid. A foundation must be solid to support the continuing loads placed on top as the entity grows. Without interaction from the client, the outside expert is denied a reasonable foundation and can only be doomed to failure. With a correct understanding of role and function for the consultant, you can build this relationship into a profitable, equitable situation. True value of a consultant results from the bidirectional information flow. It is only with your wholehearted cooperation that an advisor from outside may bring additional benefits to your installations.

Internal Staff

In considering the role of a consultant, you must not overlook the potentialities available within your staff. Frequently the best suggestions may come from the existing organization, using facilities on hand. To draw from this resource, you need to encourage a ready flow of suggestions. In making a suggested improvement to operating methods or procedures, you or your staff will be going against "the way we have always done this." This represents a subtle challenge to authority which you can utilize and put to good use.

For suggestions to flow freely in an organization, there must be an open atmosphere of acceptance. For some internal methods and procedures, the formal suggestion box may be unsatisfactory. An open meeting with a give-and-take atmosphere may encourage the most introverted programmer to propose methods and suggestions overlooked in the past. It is not enough to have the suggestions come rolling in. The new proposals must be considered, and a reply must be given to the originator. An employee who has proposed a new method deserves the courtesy and respect of an answer, accepting or rejecting the proposal and giving logical reasons for the negative decision, if any. It is not enough to reject any suggestion because of impracticality or expense. By encouraging an employee to make recommendations, you are exposing a worker to the possibility of ridicule, laughter, and even worse, prospects for ignoring the proposal in its entirety. Likewise, there may be jeers and derogatory comments from the peer group. A proposal may be rejected out-of-hand, but even so there must be valid reasons for rejection.

If a suggestion has been found worthwhile, the maker of the proposal should be given open and formal acknowledgment of a valid contribution. An open compliment serves two purposes: (1) it encourages the entire group to make proposals for reward and acknowledgment; and (2) it recognizes a contribution made by an individual. Sometimes public praise for an employee may be worth more than a cash award.

If your staff is motivated and inspired to do a competent, professional job, they will be alert for possibilities to improve the operation. Many years ago, IBM used the advertising slogan—"There must be a better way." Be it paper flow, work documentation, or programming methods, your staff is, and should be, on the alert for a better way of producing a given amount of work in a particular time frame. The same rules and practices in utilizing suggestions should be of even more significance within the confines of a shop. Inside this group, acceptable suggestions should be considered as evidence of an attempt to do a better job, to improve overall systems performance, and to make points at annual review time. In making a proposal, an employee is questioning the "accepted" way and going against the grain of authority. This may create an uneasy situation, but it can be turned into an asset. If you are fortunate enough to have a staff, then the number of assets is truly increased. When hiring and assembling this staff, you should consider not only contributions for individual efforts, but also the synergy involved when diverse personalities are brought together in a cohesive group. Internal subtleties of the group are more powerful than an individual. The free flow of suggestions within the group should be much encouraged, for the combined flow will be greater than any individual effort.

If a staff member does contribute a suggestion, it must be acknowledged. The easiest way to foster feelings of unimportance is through neglect or seeming indifference. Some suggestions may be patently unacceptable for many reasons; reasons only you may understand entirely. Frequently management has already considered and rejected various proposals due to internal considerations not apparent to your staff. There can be no excuse for ignoring a suggestion. 'Tis better to reject than overlook. Ignoring a proposal can be tantamount to stifling creativity in your staff. The creative urge, nurtured and promoted, produces more and better workable ideas than any decree from management. The surest process for eliminating idea flow from bottom to top is to adopt good ideas, implement valuable suggestions, and pass them off as your own. This is not honest and will stop the flow as effectively as a natural disaster. The talents of a manager are enhanced by efforts of the staff. It becomes your duty to encourage them—in the long run their efforts add to your stature.

Review Questions

1.   Name five automatic functions in your surroundings that contribute to personal comfort.

2.   A user department, usually very dependable for quality input, has developed bad and careless work habits which are affecting the computer production. How are you to:

(a) determine the source?

(b) correct the problem?

(c) follow-up after corrective action?

3.   A data processing consultant has been asked to visit your operation and report back to management with recommendations. Is this friend or foe?

4.   Some members of your staff are constantly making suggestions for improvements. Many of these ideas have been previously submitted and discarded. How are you tactfully going to make them aware of this fact and at the same time encourage the continuing flow of ideas?

chapter 16

Purchasing for
Data Processing

In many, if not most, small- and medium-sized installations, the duty of purchasing supplies becomes an additional task for the manager. This is brought about by the absence of a purchasing department and/or the lack of technical expertise required for defining requirements of a data processing installation. Company purchasing agents may be reluctant to learn terms and practices for dealing with a new breed of vendors, so you may be expected to absorb the entire process—defining requirements, interviewing vendors, placing of purchase orders, etc.

By assuming the role of purchasing agent, you have gained a tighter degree of control over your installation at the expense of time and potential exposure to danger or fraud. In absorbing the time required for interviewing potential vendors, available time for managing has been reduced. Many managements have no valid idea concerning the costs for supplying an installation. You may be expected to "do the best you can" and proceed with no formal instructions or minimum requirements. There were notable instances in 1977 where the exposure to fraud became too great, and a manager apparently succumbed to temptation. To avoid this potential risk, you would do well to conduct all vendor relations in the most exemplary manner.

To minimize the impact of DP purchasing, you may resort to the option of requiring all potential vendors to call for scheduled appointments on a given day. This may interfere with the agent's plans, but you are the customer—potentially. By scheduling time, you have automatically increased your own effective time management. It may be necessary to require all bids to be submitted in writing. These bids should be maintained in a file ready for inspection by auditors, internal or external. It also provides information to be used in determining vendor creditability.

Costs for establishing and maintaining an effective computer installation may be divided (roughly) into three major categories:

1. Equipment.
2. Personnel.
3. Supplies.

Of these, the area most susceptible to fraud is that of supplies. Monthly statements for equipment and payroll records for employees are always available for inspection by outsiders. With many vendors supplying diverse products, supplies offers the greatest potential for theft and fraud. In all of your dealings, you must conduct your business with integrity.

Vendor Relationships

Supervising a small installation frequently carries the additional duties of dealing with the many vendors associated with data processing. Somehow or other, representatives of accessory suppliers and business forms companies seem to be able to "smell" new installations and start making frequent calls. This task is their job, and they will serve your purposes though perhaps not in the manner envisioned when you took the job. In discussing the representatives, we should perhaps categorize them by function:

1. Equipment.
2. Accessories.
3. Forms.
4. Other supplies.

Equipment (IBM). Your most familiar equipment supplier is your friendly IBM representative. Representing one of the famous Fortune 500, he has more options for selling equipment than you have available for purchasing. Whatever your needs for data processing, IBM will have a solution. Your duty is to know and understand actual needs and what is available in the marketplace. The IBM rep is well-trained, skilled in techniques of selling, and knowledgeable about the marketplace. Maintaining a relationship with this person is an absolute necessity in managing your installation. IBM is directly interested in the welfare of your installation. IBM is concerned about other companies in your industry who do *not* have an installed IBM computer. Success or failure of your installation may have economic effects upon their marketing program. This intense interest in success is to your advantage. Maintain this relationship;

it is definitely for your benefit. IBM has many resources, perhaps too many to effectively summarize here. It is the responsibility of the IBM salesperson to furnish you with all available information necessary for successful continuance of your shop. This duty does not end with the purchase or lease of equipment.

In addition to the equipment, IBM also offers a complete line of diskettes, disk packs, the Series 1, computer cards, magnetic tapes, and a fabulous list of program products. This list does not include additional items offered through the other divisions such as typewriters, copiers, and word processing equipment. Picking and choosing from this list of "goodies" is not an easy task. As a DP manager and purchasing agent, your selection is made easier because many of these products are not in the System 3 product line. The consumable types of products (diskettes, cards, etc.) are excellent quality and guaranteed to meet all specifications for satisfactory performance.

Program products offered by IBM include compilers, sorts, and a system control program. The system control program is an extremely powerful operating system. All of these products have been through an extensive, costly development period and are suitable for the end-user. If a shop is experiencing growth problems operating with a limited, inexperienced staff, there are additional program products designed and built to fill this specific need. Field-developed programs, or installed user programs, were developed in the field by an IBM-er or customer, and are intended to fill exact, specific application needs. FDP's may not be 100% usable without modification, and occasionally there are some blank spaces in basic assumptions. For the most part, these purchased programs will fill user needs more quickly and economically than an internally developed, user-written program.

There are other manufacturers of peripheral gear for the System 3. These sources offer a fairly complete line of printers, data recorders, disk drives, and add-on memory. Usually most prices for lease or purchase are considerably lower than equivalent IBM prices. Performance and capacity are usually improved over the IBM counterpart. As a small system manager becomes more knowledgeable about different options that are available, these suppliers may offer viable alternatives.

In considering the usage of non-IBM gear, the most important considerations should be: (1) Will it do the job? and (2) What are the arrangements for customer engineering service? It is false economy to reduce hardware costs and later realize that the equipment does not perform as represented, or that repair parts and service must be imported from outside the state. If your installation is removed from a major metropolitan area or city, you would do well to consider very carefully any choice of non-IBM gear. Similar to the advertising campaigns of Sears or General Electric, IBM strives to service (well) what they sell.

Accessories and Supplies. With the installation of your computer comes the need for accessories. There will be a real need for chairs, tables, and other office items. Some specialized needs will be determined by an exact configuration, but for the most part there are basic items that must be purchased and made a normal part of office furniture and fixtures. Data entry operators may require a small desk or table for temporary storage of personal effects and procedure manuals. It may be desirable to have a special rack on the computer console to contain manuals necessary for machine operation and problem solutions. Specialized file cabinets for cards, diskettes, and disk packs may be necessary. A supply of ribbons for the printer, and other peripherals, will be needed. Continuous forms may require shelving of some type. If report output is of sufficient volume, there may be need for a carbon decollator and burster. Some installations also use an electric time clock for time-stamping work in and out. For every need there is at least one supplier, probably two or more.

In considering the purchase of any of these items, you would do well to define your needs very carefully. There are many manufacturers and sales representatives who are happy to assist in the specification writing. This is usually done in the hope and expectation of receiving the order. A vendor who is willing to perform this task will also write the specifications so as to remove the competition from consideration. Many manufacturers will allow more than one local company to market their products, thereby allowing each marketer some flexibility in setting prices. By working with a carefully written shopping list and interviewing more than one supplier, a manager should be able to satisfy immediate needs—at a most favorable price.

In selecting a container—cabinet or safe—for some items, care must be taken to insure suitability of purpose. If there are elements of data security, caution should be used in purchasing cabinets or files without limited provision for protection against fire damage and unauthorized access to files, programs, disks, etc. At first comparison, additional costs for locks may appear to be unreasonable. Certainly, the greater expense of a fireproof safe is going to represent a significant increase over costs for "sheltering" files. Management may elect to consider fire as an acceptable risk if you have allowed for offsite-storage of backup records and files. The original costs for locks and fire-resistant or fireproof protection are almost negligible when spread over expected life of the equipment. If your files contain valuable programs and proprietary data, or the loss of files would severely restrict the company's ability to operate, then the need for a secure file becomes a necessity—not just a nice-to-have option. Selection of a safe should include an allowance for possible future needs. By opting for satisfaction of immediate requirements, future growth needs may be overlooked. Decisions should be based upon consideration of a combination of potential risk factors including fire, floods, or other natural disasters, and the more distinct possibility of human intervention. Off-premises storage provides a service that will satisfy more dire threats, but it does not remove danger potential completely. A careful mixing of factors will provide necessary storage and meet the requirements for data security, satisfying more than one requirement at a manageable additional cost.

There are many sources of supply for I/O equipment ribbons. Ribbons are available from IBM, office supply houses, or accessory dealers. Some specialized ribbons are available only from the equipment vendor or specialized supply houses. Some IBM equipment requires an inked ribbon cartridge available only through IBM. This is considered to be an exclusive, but in many instances ribbon manufacturers were reluctant to manufacture within the specifications for a minimum tolerance. To be on the safe side, order your ribbons from a supplier who will furnish the best combination of price and service. To ensure a fresh ribbon supply, inventory requirements should not exceed projected usage for a period of six months. Private label suppliers will market ribbons under many brand names, local and national. To avoid extensive, costly analyses of lines printed per ribbon, it is wise to record ribbon changes on the production log, thus allowing at least a cursory examination of usage and elapsed calendar time. Special unexpected production runs with many pages of print will seriously affect anticipated ribbon life. Re-inking services are available for most printer ribbons, but this does require saving of ribbons and going through the process of pickup and delivery. You must determine whether this service will satisfactorily meet your needs.

To ensure the professional appearance of printer output, it is wise to change ribbons frequently to produce a consistently crisp, clear impression. Appearance of the report may not add to value, but it adds to the impression made on the end-user. In terms of print lines, a ribbon should be considered a part of total report cost, and is an extremely minor part of contributed costs. Ribbons, any size, any style, should be considered a part of machine costs and changed readily. The cost for computer ribbons is relatively much less than comparable ribbons for typewriters and adding machines.

Selecting the Forms Supplier. The choice of a major supplier to be charged with the responsibility for meeting most forms needs should be made very carefully. Custom forms, such as checks, invoices, or statements, are visible representatives of your employer and should carry the impression of a quality product. The principal vendor will be required to work closely with you to understand and determine your exact needs. Between customer and supplier there is a close business relationship. It may take time to develop this working relationship, but it is worth it. For example, if you have an established base of custom forms and stock, the sales representative can be invaluable in suggesting various combinations for ordering and selecting forms sizes. Also, if your forms inventory inadvertently falls beneath the order point, you can ask for expedited delivery and an accelerated production schedule. On the vendor's behalf, if all continuous form requirements are met through an established policy of accepting the absolute lowest bid, there is no justification for the user to expect extra services.

Selection of one major supplier should not exclude the maintenance of alternate sources of supply. During the paper shortage in the early 1970's, many users were forced to search for additional sources of supply. Without an established network of suppliers, new sources were limited. By maintaining more than one source, the user also is able to keep all suppliers "honest" in maintaining a reasonable cost structure.

A DP installation manager should not spend laborious hours carefully designing a form, specifying each technical requirement for the printer. It is more efficient to rough out general needs, submit them to your forms supplier and ask for a detailed presentation for meeting your requirements and incorporating suggestions for lowering forms costs. A reputable supplier should make specific recommendations involving weight of paper, choice of inks, fastening methods, and be aware of additional forms handling requirements *after* processing. By combining the efforts of customer and manufacturer, forms costs can be managed and kept within an acceptable minimum.

There are accepted industry standards for paper sizes to be used in the production of continuous forms. The familiar letter-size of 8½" wide by 11" long is a typical example of standardization. By restricting forms sizes to a standard multiple of 11 inches, you have options for other forms applications with little additional cost. Eleven-inch forms may be conveniently divided into multiples of 5½" or 3⅔". There are also 7-inch presses allowing for 7 or 14 inches, or reasonable multiples of in-between sizes. Your supplier is, or should be, expected to steer you into effective sizes.

Forms Considerations. Before perfection of pin-feed tractors and carriages, some very early unit-record equipment used rolls of unperforated paper similar to a roll of adding machine tape, only wider and longer. Today, continuous forms with perforated margins and scored slitting at top and bottom offer the only convenient way of keeping a ready supply of forms in the printer. Different combinations of paper sizes and weights, with and without carbon, carbon blackouts on inside copies, and the possibilities of multiple-ply forms, offer a wide range of user options. The two basic choices are for "stock" paper and the so-called "customized" form. Stock paper is available from most suppliers in relatively set sizes and ply combinations. Stock may be lined or unlined, depending upon the manufacturers' decisions as to what is considered to be off-the-shelf stock. A customized form will include certain items such as a company logo, columns and tabular headings, boxes for totals or account numbers, page numbers, including any customer requirements for colors or extra printing on the reverse side of the form. In most instances, a custom form will be more expensive than a stock form.

Continuous forms are generally marketed by three types of representatives. There may be other combinations, but the basic types are:

1. Manufacturers' representatives of local or national firm.
2. Jobbers or brokers representing many available sources of supply.
3. Office supply houses also representing a printing outlet.

For your purposes, it is wise to consider all three sources as potential suppliers because each will offer differing amounts of expertise and knowledge. To a large extent, you may expect manufacturers and jobbers or brokers to offer the most expertise and knowledge in meeting your forms needs. Some office supply houses are excellent choices for forms, but frequently may lack the necessary special skill for assisting you in designing and determining forms needs.

National forms companies have extensive resources of printing plants, paper suppliers, and distribution systems. Their sales forces are well-trained and bring the capabilities of a strong organization to bear in meeting exacting requirements. Original prices come from a catalog or fixed price list, but local agents may have a limited amount of flexibility in deviating from the fixed price. The forms industry is highly competitive in prices and services offered to the user. Large national firms offer art services, a wide range of printing inks, screened pantographs, and samples of special forms which may give you valuable hints in layout and design of an effective form.

The local jobber represents several available factories which produce forms on a contract basis. Some of these factories will have their representatives in designated territories and use brokers in areas considered to be uneconomical for maintaining a full office staff. This representative is working with relatively fixed production costs, markup being determined by the amount of gross profit needed to stay in business. Many of these independents were trained by the national firms and have solid experience. With a comprehensive number of suppliers, the jobber can pick or choose firms offering desirable combinations of press sizes and delivery schedules. This can result in lower cost for the user. With no control over suppliers, the independent forms representative may be faced with problems of quality control, though most facilities are interested in maintaining high standards for production schedules and supplying users with a quality product or form.

Review Questions

1.   By assuming the role of purchasing agent for an installation, you are obligating yourself to spend time interviewing vendors. Is this the way to run a computer installation? If not, who should assume these duties?

2.   IBM has been very persistent in sales efforts to convince you of the need for additional equipment. You have agreed, but feel that a management presentation is required. Who should make the presentation?

3.   Assuming continuous forms requirements of (over) $1,000 per month average, how many suppliers should be involved in your account? Discuss variations in forms suppliers.

4.   Management insists upon purchase orders being awarded to the lowest bidder. Service and delivery have been problems in the past. Justify your decision to award a forms contract to someone other than the low bidder.

chapter 17

Motivation and Leadership

The terms *motivation* and *leadership* are representative of qualities that only you, the supervisor, can bring to your staff. Both qualities are easy to define and evaluate. The task of supplying leadership and motivation is a more difficult job. There are many excellent books, papers, and serious articles concerning each topic. Relatively few of these treatises even attempt to suggest a method for developing these qualities. Many of these works can name various leaders who were able to supply necessary, and needed, motivation and leadership as required by circumstances. Quite interestingly, these books produce a "phantom" list (by omission) of other leaders who did not possess these same attributes. Certain characteristics are common to all good leaders, and some of these qualities are present in varying degrees at all levels of management.

As a supervisor of personnel and equipment, you are expected to supply a form of motivation. Other than an occasional lubrication of moving parts, equipment does not require much motivation to ensure satisfactory performance of an assigned task. Personnel, though not requiring lubrication with a petroleum product, must be encouraged and motivated to perform their jobs according to expectations. Failure to consider staff members as something other than robots doing mechanically defined tasks will lead to a breakdown of the personnel relationship.

As with so many other management tasks, there is no pat answer or technique to be applied in any and all situations. There are many excellent publications, all of which contribute to a greater understanding and awareness of problems in motivation and leadership. Even with a greater awareness, you may have a difficult time applying all principles discussed in each book. What you do must be a reflection of your personal style of management and supervision. Some very basic ideas and thoughts for successful motivation are described in subsequent paragraphs. These suggestions are "how to" in nature and do not cover all aspects. Use the ones applicable to your situation and adapt the others on an "as-needed" basis. Develop your own style, never forgetting the fact you were once a subordinate reporting to a supervisor. Your success will be measured in good morale and low employee turnover.

Individual Respect

One of the prime interests concerning employees is your attitude about the individual. Each individual carries inculcated values, traditions, and an amount of self-esteem and personal dignity. Actions taken as a group leader should never infringe nor degrade the employee's personal values. An individual in your employ is looking, or searching, for a comfortable place to work and be recognized as a person. How you react to personalities and interoffice relationships will determine an employee's acceptance of your position as a leader. Perhaps you represent an authoritarian figure, or just the opposite—an easy-going personality with not a care in the world. Your role is to provide an image of confidence with assurance the problems will always work out.

As a supervisor, you may tend to ignore your position as the "boss." The people who are working for you will never forget. To them, you are the company, the source of their jobs, and they are extremely interested and involved in earning your approval. Likewise, you must be earnest and diligent in earning respect from them. By treating everyone with dignity, respect, and equality, you will go far in earning your position (in their minds) as a supervisor.

Job Satisfaction

Each individual is working for some amount of monetary reward and an intangible amount of personal job satisfaction. For many employees, job fulfillment meets an internal need undefined in any book. Jobs are switched for relatively small amounts of money, sometimes even a decrease in pay. Reasons for this change may be traced back to a need for job gratification. Few employees are willing to admit, or even recognize, this need for job satisfaction. It is not a characteristic found in all employees in equal measure. This urge for happiness may surpass all monetary rewards, perhaps even family needs.

It is a personal challenge for you to recognize this inner need of your staff. The management task is to recognize this desire and translate it into effective job performance. In doing so, you may make shifts in job assignments or work duties in an attempt to bring out this personal sense of fulfillment. Some employees construe difficult work assignments as a form of praise, though this is not true for all situations. Others enjoy the thrill of completing an assigned task and enjoying a sense of achievement. The job facing the supervisor is to provide the personal rewards that satisfy this need for personal contentment.

Techniques of Conversation

The most effective conversationalist is a good listener. To discover how your employees feel about their job and company, and almost every other subject, try asking questions and listening to the answers. Any individual enjoys the sound of his or her own voice and welcomes a willing ear.

Do not be surprised about the information that you will learn through conversation. Many times a supervisor will pick up vague notions of employee discontent or unrest. Frequently, this knowledge is gleaned by a careful examination of what was not said. Confidentiality of some conversations must be protected. Employees who are encouraged to visit with their immediate boss will develop a rapport for the job and work situation. These conversations may be brief and infrequent. As a good (but experienced) listener, you should also use this opportunity as a method of explaining company policy, decisions, and clearing up any confusion which may exist only in the employee's mind.

Be very careful not to devote all conversational efforts toward only limited members of the staff. This would lead to real employee dissatisfaction. Without using a checklist, all members of the group should have some opportunity to visit with you. Productive time may be lost, but feelings of personal loyalty will be increased. Talking with each employee is one of the most effective means of building a cohesive group of employees.

Personal Growth and Advancement

Most employees are concerned about future potential of the job and possibilities for personal growth and advancement. Over a period of time, the nature of the position will change, and an employee deserves to know what his or her future role could be. To tell an employee that the chances for personal growth and real advancement are extremely limited is to smother or diminish a striving for an improved situation. Some job positions may not allow for much growth. This is no reason why a job should not be considered the stepping stone to be used for promotion.

Advancement is an increase in job status and personal satisfaction, with or without monetary reward. As such, job titles are somewhat meaningless. It is not considered good practice to hand out job titles which do not represent a true advancement of status. A promotion is reward for past duties effectively performed and encouragement for even more successful efforts in the future. Such changes should be real, and infrequent enough so that there is no loss of appeal for motivating other employees.

Personal Traits

A manager may, and should, notice the appearance of all employees on a daily basis. If a female employee changes her hair style to one more attractive, by all means tell her so. Male employees who appear at work in a new tie or outfit that improves their appearance should also be complimented. This not only increases an employee's self-esteem, but also lets them know that you are interested in them as people.

Be careful not to overdo the compliments on frequent changes in clothing or hair styles. By overemphasizing every change, an employee will lose confidence in the sincerity of the compliment. Your notice should be a blending of personal interest in appearance and sincere compliments on beneficial changes or improvements.

There are negative personal traits which deserve personal attention from the supervisor. These circumstances must be handled with the most delicate care. Many of these situations may be covered in a company policy manual or dress code. For those that are not mentioned in policy manuals, the utmost diplomacy is required for careful managing of the problem. Rather than singling out one employee for personal attention, it may be desirable to have a group meeting and bring the topic into general consideration. If only one individual is the serious offender, the situation must be privately and confidentially handled in order to avoid embarrassing anyone in a peer group.

As a manager or supervisor, you must use extreme caution in discussing or mentioning negative factors about an employee's personal traits or appearance. Better results are achieved through the open playing-up of positive factors and the quiet, subtle encouragement from other employees to reduce or improve those negative factors which detract from the real person.

Monetary Compensation

Money is no longer considered to be a prime motivation for an employee. Compensation for any position must or should be on a par with like positions in the industry or community. Inequities resulting from gross pay differences will contribute to high employee turnover and unrest. Money does afford a tangible reward for job accomplishments. As a motivator, money may be gratefully accepted; *reasons* for an increase will serve as the real impetus for continuing more-than-satisfactory on-the-job performance.

The internal grapevine of any organization will spread news of a salary increase much faster than publishing increases in the company newspaper. This is true regardless of company policy concerning the discussing of pay rates and increases. In turn, this self-same discussion may result in a drop of employee morale ("why didn't I get a raise also?"). The competent supervisor is ready for this question (formal or informal), and should assure all staff members of fair and equitable consideration at the correct time. Equal pay for equal work is a valid standard in the establishment of pay schedules. If questions of inequality arise, a supervisor must have valid reasons for maintaining pay differentials on certain jobs. Years of experience may be valid to some extent, but does not provide an excuse for significant differences in pay. Several levels within a job classification are acceptable, providing the different steps are carefully defined.

Involvement in Decision-making

Very few employees enjoy being treated as a cipher or just another face on the assembly line. Decisions affecting an employee's well-being are usually made at a high management level without individual employee involvement. These decrees, when handed down, may create employee dissatisfaction and lowered morale. Corporate edicts may be handled this way, but a computer room supervisor would do better by announcing internal resolutions on a more personal level. The ultimate determination is still up to the manager, but it is possible to use this method as a means of gathering employee support.

In delivering a decision to your staff, you increase their acceptance of your role as a manager by asking for continuing support and suggestions. Your subordinates, if encouraged, should be allowed to consider and comment on the implications of decisions affecting their jobs and work situations. An autocratic approach will be needed for portions of a management edict, though some points of contention should be considered and discussed. This is similar to the principles of user involvement (when planning new applications) and carries the same rewards of cooperation.

Most employees enjoy the privilege of having their input considered as part of the decision-making process. Free discussion will disclose the reasons behind the decision and allow the opportunity to justify selected elements of the decision. This does not imply the employees can change or overrule a management edict. Unannounced and undiscussed decrees affecting groups of employees may meet with resistance. A reasonable explanation of decision considerations and alternatives provides a management sounding-board for reasonable justification and implementation of decisions.

Negative Motivation

Many factors, internal and external, can contribute to a decline in employee efficiency and production. Some are personal, such as family disagreement, children's behavior, pressure of unpaid bills, illness, or almost anything else which affects an employee personally. The alert manager will pay close attention to those symptoms which are manifested by employee behavior.

Tardiness or absenteeism on the part of a heretofore dependable employee may be outward symptoms of a more severe problem not yet surfaced. A drop in production rates or the missing of schedules may represent a mind distracted by personal problems. The introduction of careless errors into work flow should also serve as a warning flag to the supervisor. Before taking any disciplinary action, the manager would do well to visit at length with the employee. Frequently, this first level of counseling will provide an employee the moral support necessary to identify the problem and talk it out. Many troublesome situations may be resolved through the efforts of a concerned manager. If the problem is beyond your capabilities as a supervisor, it should be referred to the personnel department or an agency which specializes in such matters. The drastic step of employee termination should be considered only after sources of aid have been exhausted.

Motivation Summary

The many factors affecting the psychological makeup of an employee are too numerous to effectively catalogue or mention here. An awareness of factors contributing to the success or failure of an employee to perform satisfactorily on the job will make your job as a manager much easier. Your skills at supplying the motivation, and informal counseling, may provide an employee with the reason for continuing to work satisfactorily at a high level of enthusiasm and performance. A personal interest in, and attention to, the welfare of your staff will contribute to the creating and maintaining of an efficient staff.

Leadership

As an appointed manager, you are expected and assumed to possess qualities of leadership. These attributes are rarely defined in the job description. As previously discussed, motivation must be supplied to staff members. Inspiration must come from within and permeate the entire department. The confidence in self, staff, and equipment lends an aura of managerial competence. A leader must be friendly with the staff, not displaying favoritism, and not becoming overly familiar with any employee. The capable manager, using honest encouragement, will convince all employees that they are working together for a common benefit. Loyalty to the department and operation will flow from leaders to followers and then back again. All of this must be combined with a demeanor indicating total and complete control of the situation. Rather than discussing the composition of leadership traits, you should be concerned with displaying those characteristics which contribute to your role as a leader.

Confidence

A supervisor must possess great amounts of confidence in the capabilities of staff, equipment, and himself. This air of conviction must be readily apparent to all having contact within the installation. Your staff should be able to sense or feel this belief and faith in reinforcing their beliefs and expectations. This is a bi-directional relationship, and you should expect this same confidence flowing upward. It may require time and effort to develop this flow. Success has been achieved when the entire shop is knowledgeable and confident about their position in the operation. This certainty gives strength to the installation.

A public display of confidence may be a facade, or it may approach a degree of conceit. A manager must possess, at all times, an assurance of self that supports the operation. By assuming the air of command audacity, it is possible to develop confidence into a strong attitude that becomes reality.

Attitude

A director of data processing must constantly display a positive attitude. Part of this attitude is reflected in the show of confidence mentioned earlier. By maintaining a rather consistent demeanor, you will communicate this stability to the entire group. A supervisor is not expected to exhibit human traits of a "bad mood" or a "blue Monday." You would do well to leave all personal feelings at home and endeavor to present a constant (pleasing) demeanor to the outside world. In remaining seemingly unaffected by outside forces, this will contribute to a positive point of view for the installation. This steady effort will have the value of pulling the office into a closely knit working team.

Favoritism and Encouragement

An administrator will devote equal time and attention to the needs of all employees. It may be a difficult task at times to avoid paying excessive amounts of consideration to one individual. Some workers thrive with attention from the boss. Other staff members seem to do better with less attention from the manager. Still other employees will use every opportunity to gain influence. The skilled manager will tread the tightrope between excessive attention and disinterest.

Unquestionably, you may develop a stronger sense of rapport and support with some key individuals among your staff. The individuals may be concerned with promotion or job advancement. As a result, they may show an increased attention to satisfactory performance on the job. Enthusiasm for getting the work done should be lauded and praised openly. This may provide an incentive for other employees to pay closer attention to their work performance.

In your efforts to stimulate and encourage staff members to strive for achievement, do not overlook the possibilities of constructive praise and criticism. This commendation does support past efforts and lets all workers know of your interest in their welfare. Praise should be delivered openly in the presence of others. Comments or observations indicating a less-than-satisfactory standard of work should be handled with no other staff members listening. This may take place in a review session or over a brief cup of coffee. Most times, an employee is very aware of his or her production. Your efforts in praising or criticizing this employee may have the desired effect of turning a less than average worker into a valuable member of the team.

Working – With or For

Does your staff work for you, or with you? If your operators and programmers are working *for* you, the office may be losing valuable time and production. Successful managers create an atmosphere of working *with* the staff. The autocratic leader may demand and receive an exceptional standard level of production. An overseer who is more indulgent in style can develop a united team approach, more effective for production and the maintenance of a high level of morale.

Individuals enjoy the feeling of belonging to a group. This is even more true in a work situation. If there is a barrier between worker and boss that is seemingly like the Iron Curtain, an employee may develop feelings of resentment concerning management—immediate supervisors included. In allying your interests with those of the group, it becomes much easier to ask for their continuing support when "we have a problem." For example, if management orders the staff to stay late and produce a report, the authority contained in orders is likely to be resented. The capable manager will *ask* the group to stay late to produce the needed information. By saying, "We have a problem, and we need your help on a special project tonight," the supervisor has shouldered much of the responsibility and indicated a willingness to work with the group. It remains a very effective means for developing team togetherness in your computer installation. This team support is most beneficial when the crew is working with you, and you with them.

Loyalty

In working for an organization, many workers develop a sense of loyalty to the company, and more importantly, to the individual department and supervisor. This sense of belonging or allegiance can produce side benefits when utilized for your purposes. It is desirable to encourage and support those activities which contribute to this need for belonging. Loyalty is not an ingrained part of the department. It is earned respect and is an outer display of inner feelings. Inside the shop your staff may laugh and joke about errors and production rates. Within the confines of an installation, errors and production rates may be common problems. If an outsider mentions this same problem in a derogatory fashion, the entire staff may take personal offense at this criticism. This display of departmental loyalty reflects the strong feeling of the combined group. An insult to one is an insult to all. Your function as a departmental leader is to encourage the development of departmental and personal loyalty. Without this cohesive feeling, it may be more difficult to develop a working team.

Loyalty as a trait is not reserved solely for the workers under your control. Loyalty flows in both directions. It is a matter of departmental pride that you extend the same amount of loyalty to your subordinates. In looking to you for guidance and support, an employee must receive equal amounts of loyalty. You do not let other department heads criticize any of your workers. As a matter of fact, when justified, you go to the outsiders and offer high praises for the quality of production coming from such an effective and competent staff (yours). This builds a sense of loyalty and belonging that other organizations will envy.

Loyalty is an intangible asset, part of the mortar, that holds the formal and informal organization together. Pay close attention to this asset. It makes for a strong department and work force.

Review Questions

1. Famous leaders of history are listed below. Describe each in terms of leadership and motivation:

(a) Lucretia Borgia

(b) Machiavelli

(c) General Douglas MacArthur

(d) Adolph Hitler

(e) Abraham Lincoln

(f) Martin Luther King

(g) Helen Keller

2. In your own terms, what are you working toward, and where will you be in the next five, ten, and twenty years?

3. Do you owe your subordinates loyalty? If so, give an example.

chapter 18

Your Relationship
with IBM

The relationship with your major vendor will have a continuing effect upon the success of the installation. To be sure, your shop may be comparatively insignificant when measured against the real dollars of a very large complex. In reality, however, the size of IBM has little effect upon your installation. The marketing representative is financially concerned about the success of your shop, for he knows that a well-managed installation will be a good customer. Behind this sales effort is a veritable army of customer engineers, systems representatives, branch office administrative personnel, and the corporate structure of IBM.

You are not the only customer. Each installed account represents a continuing source of revenue to IBM. It is to their best interests, at all levels, to make resources available to each customer. There are various levels of support personnel which contribute to the continuing success of your installation. As a matter of practice, you will have more frequent contact with major front-line support in the form of the systems representative and the customer engineer. There are others who insure the delivery of manuals, hardware, etc., but your most frequent dealings will be with field and sales support personnel. Each support person will play an important role in the growth and development of your installation.

The Marketing Representative

The man or woman charged with account responsibility is the most prominent representative of IBM. This person is charged with the duty not only for the original sale, but also for the continuation of a good business relationship between the customer and IBM. There are elements of profit in this duty, but marketing duties do not end with hardware installation and collection of a commission check. This person has the duty of ensuring the overall success of the account. This includes coordinating delivery schedules and recommendations for physical planning. Program products, such as sorts and compilers, must be ordered in advance of delivery. Coding sheets for programs must be made available; education courses and schedules must be considered; and management must be constantly reassured of the wisdom of acquiring a computer from IBM. Necessary support manuals and documentation must be listed and ordered. Internally, IBM requires a comprehensive amount of paperwork and coordination for manufacturing and marketing resources. The entire process is designed to assure the customer of a smooth installation with little left to chance. This procedure produces internal benefits for IBM, though the customer is the main recipient of dividends.

For successful marketing the sales representative must be made aware of industry requirements. This has resulted in the creation of industry specialists. By training and experience, this has enhanced the possibilities for marketing success. If your firm is in the distribution industry, your sales representative is quite knowledgeable about general industry problems and indeed may know more specifics than you do. A marketing representative is also responsible for the continuing growth of your installation.

There are publications and papers in the IBM archives detailing the many different approaches for installation management and development that have been successful in the past. Your job is to draw upon every potential source of information that may be helpful in creating a successful shop. Be encouraged to use the resources of IBM in your march toward success. The sales rep should also serve as the spokesperson between you and other IBM divisions.

The Data Processing Divison of IBM, being bigger and older than GSD (General Systems Division), has a much larger library of application write-ups and other publications written to help facilitate the implementation of software, hardware, and—perhaps more importantly—extensive applications studies which may be of benefit in your planning for the future.

In short, the salesperson represents IBM, not only to you, but also to your employer. Use this sales talent and accompanying resources to smooth your job and relations with management. New applications may be developed on paper and measured against prior experiences in other installations, thus allowing a semi-audit against known successes. The salesperson is concerned with success of IBM and the installation in that order. Any suggestions or contributions will be tailored toward the growth of both entities. Some of this help will be garnered from past experiences and should be used with discretion and judgment.

Systems Representatives

A systems representative is the person who provides the technical support for leased program products (utilities, sorts, compilers, and purchased program products) and for the IBM-supplied software necessary for operation of the equipment. As a source of information for understanding and knowledge of successful machine utilization, the systems representative offers a world of experiences from many installations.

The SE (systems engineer) can make helpful suggestions for implementation, and just as readily, offer warnings of potential problems. Not to overlook or deny the wealth of information contained in IBM publications, a knowledgeable SE is, or has been, exposed to many other customers and situations. Many of these experiences are not detailed in any manual, and the customer may not be aware of dangers lurking in proposed new applications.

It is not necessary nor effective to have the SE on site at all times in the small installation. If you are supervising your operation in an effective manner, the SE should only be needed on an occasional basis, providing assistance only on an emergency or one-time problem basis. For this reason, you should have established a working relationship with the SE so he or she understands the configuration, the applications, personal limitations of staff, and the entire installation. Only in this fashion can some problems be resolved over the telephone or by a brief visit.

Maintain good relations with your assigned SE. Like your staff, an SE enjoys a pleasant situation and will spend time where he or she is warmly received. Even if the SE is only making a courtesy call, take the time and visit for a while. This will bring new applications up-to-date, and you have the opportunity to mention how you have solved other problems. Frequently, you will be the recipient of more recommendations for minimizing future delays of implementation. You cannot expect the SE to do productive programming or systems design without a contract for systems engineering services. Interviewing and a lively question-and-answer session can provide more services than any program written by an SE.

Customer Engineer and Technical Specialists

Occasionally, a computer will develop an ailment, and the software will tend to reject a user-written program. Machine ailments require the attention of the customer engineer. Using your description of the symptoms and apparent failure, the CE (customer engineer) will define the problem area and apply various diagnostic techniques to remedy and correct hardware problems. If the problem is with an IBM-supplied piece of software, a technical specialist may be required. There are occasions when roles of these two specialists overlap and become blurred. It is not your responsibility as a manager to determine which specialist will be required. Once the trouble call has been made, the CE will either solve the hardware problem or call in the specialist if the situation appears to be a software problem. There are ailments that are manifest in hardware malfunctions, but are really symptoms of a failure in software.

The customer engineer is frequently operating under something of a disagreeable handicap. Usually you will only see a CE when you are having machine troubles. Coming into your office, he or she is already at a disadvantage—the machine is malfunctioning. This is even more true since newer pieces of hardware are more reliable and require very little preventive maintenance. Do not let the apparent machine trouble affect your relationship with the CE. Later on you may find that it was "customer error" or "no trouble found." Explain the problem and encourage the CE to speedily repair the problem. Time for recrimination may be required later; the immediate problem is to return the computer to active production.

The technical specialist is (usually) an ex-CE who has served time as a field engineer and has been promoted. A tech specialist is thoroughly knowledgeable with the electromechanical problems of hardware and has been trained in the software intricacies. This combination is very helpful in determining the nature of needed repairs. An item of software may require a "fix" if you uncover legitimate shortcomings of a compiler or utility. Various IBM-supplied products, such as compilers and sorts, are not always 100% effective and may require only a minute change to function as represented. This is no job for the CE or the manager, and indeed the tech specialist is probably the only person who can recognize the problem and provide the solution.

General Technical Services

General support provided by IBM for the System 3 family of computers is excellent. There is more than adequate support at all levels to deal with almost any kind of operational problem. The engineering staff and support group are more than willing to assist the customer in maintaining a well-running installation. Support should not be measured only by the number or frequency of trouble calls. The effectiveness is measured in customer satisfaction. If there are problems of inadequate engineering assistance, everyone concerned with the account is more than anxious to remedy the situation.

As a wise public relations move, you should inform the engineering manager of your satisfaction with the engineering services and support. As mentioned earlier, the CE is usually seen only at a troublesome time. Earnest words of praise and commendation for a job well done will go far in establishing a comfortable working relationship with the support staff.

Preventive Maintenance

The striving for electronic excellence has produced equipment requiring little or no scheduled time for preventive maintenance. This is quite a contrast when measured against the older unit-record gear which was subject to much wear of mechanical parts, requiring frequent calls for equipment service.

Electronic components have no moving parts. It is true that I/O gear does have mechanical parts which are subject to normal wear and deterioration. Compared with older gear, even the need for maintenance has been considerably reduced. Printers, card readers and punches, and some motor-driven components are subject to wear and do require a certain amount of unavoidable maintenance.

As a means of reducing disruptive downtime due to a hardware failure or malfunction, preventive maintenance should be scheduled on a periodic basis. Even though the newer equipment does not require frequent inspection, the need has only been decreased, not eliminated.

If your configuration does require periodic inspection and the exercising of certain components, it is a wise investment in time to take advantage of this "insurance." Some managers are reluctant to give up their equipment to the engineer for cyclical inspection. This short-sighted approach is totally ineffective in preventing minor hardware problems from developing into major machine catastrophes at the worst possible times.

Aside from scheduled time required for manufacturer maintenance and inspection, it is excellent internal policy to adopt a "clean room" concept for the machine room. Smoking should be discouraged, and food or drink should be against all policies for the equipment facilities. Any steps or process which will minimize the introduction of foreign matter into a computer environment will aid in keeping the equipment functioning effectively over a longer period of time.

Review Questions

1. Why should IBM show a continuing interest in your installation?

2. Your sales representative comes by frequently, discussing new industry applications and urging you to push for implementation. Is this a valid approach to marketing?

3. The IBM SE assigned to your account seems to lack knowledge of your problems and the configuration. How are you to resolve this situation?

4. The hardware in your installation is showing signs of intermittent failure. Should you place a definite trouble call, or call and ask the CE to come by to check the equipment?

5. One school of thought says — as long as the equipment is running, don't fool with it. The other theory is to allow for preventive maintenance in order to minimize downtime. Which is most effective, in your opinion?

chapter 19

The System 3
Manager

If you are manager and general factotum of a small one- or two-person operation, some ideas and principles discussed in this book may not seem totally applicable for your situation. In isolated instances, this may be a valid assumption. For the most part, a small shop will need all available advice and services in establishing a successfully managed installation. The need for documentation is even more important in the small installation. Emergency backup procedures are always required regardless of installation size. Frequently, the tendency in the small shop is to disregard basic principles because "we are not big enough" or "after this next project, we will reorganize." Nothing could be more ill-advised.

As data processing manager of a System 3 installation, you will be called upon and expected to perform some rather spectacular feats. Before you attempt to leap the first building with but a single bound, you should be made aware of the definitions for *manager* and *data processing*.

The Oxford Universal Dictionary, published with addenda in 1955, contains this definition, among others: "One skilled in managing affairs, money, etc." and "one who manages a business, an institution, etc."[1] Perhaps these definitions are adequate. In rather dry and unemotional terms, they name the function, if not detailing the individual duties.

IBM goes into much more detail when the duties of a data processing manager are defined as:

Plans and directs all data processing activities of the corporation. Plans for improvements to the corporation's activities through new or improved systems. Directs the fulfillment of data processing services, development, and production. Through liaison with users of data pro-

[1] *The Oxford Universal Dictionary*, 3rd ed., revised with Addenda, 1955, (Oxford University Press, Amen House, London E.C.4)

cessing services, provides support for improving organization activities through improved methods and techniques and better utilization of resources. Organizes data processing resources to provide efficient and effective service to users.[2]

The generic term, data processing, is very simply defined in the IBM System 32 General Information publication (GC21-7582-0) as "performing a series of planned actions upon information to achieve a desired result."[3]

The definitions in simple straightforward words and phrases do not really describe the duties and responsibilities nor the complexities of managing a computer installation. As a manager, you will not be concerned with dry and dusty words. You will be concerned with unemotional equipment and live, warm people. The interpersonal relationships between you, the manager, and the staff are such that they defy cataloging by a computer of almost any size. There are too many variables, too many unknowns, to fit every situation. It is possible to further define the job, or role, of the manager by separating the general duties of the job into rather specific functions.

Combined, these job functions are symbiotic in nature. That is to say—the sum of the parts is greater than the whole. It is your prime mission to maintain these symbiotic functions as a manageable entity. Similar to a multi-headed Hydra, this is an assignment that is possible to control. To manage this assignment successfully, you should define the individual areas of responsibility. Once the problems have been listed and delineated and you are aware of the complexity, the task is not quite so formidable. Just as Rome was not built in a day, neither will you be asked to actually perform duties in each task every day. The DP manager's job consists of many facets or duties and responsibilities, some of them unrelated to the job description. In your tenure as a supervisor, you may be expected to show varying degrees of expertise in the following partial list of functions:

1. Purchasing agent.
2. Personnel interviewer.
3. Technical expert (DP).
4. Planning specialist.
5. Technical writer (documentation).

[2] *Organizing the Data Processing Activity*, 3rd ed., 1973, International Business Machines Corporation, Data Processing Division, 1133 Westchester Avenue, White Plains, New York 10604.

[3] *IBM System 32 Introduction*, International Business Machines Corporation, General Systems Division, Atlanta, Georgia 30342.

   6. Labor relations negotiations.

   7. Accounting theory.

   8. Manufacturing, expediting, and scheduling.

   9. Inventory control.

   10. Sales analysis.

   11. Credit analysis and policy.

   12. Vehicle scheduling and maintenance.

   13. Corporate policy.

   14. Vendor relations.

   15. Banking and financial relationships.

   16. Marriage counseling.

   17. ROI (return on investment) analyst.

   18. Public and community relations.

This partial list of duties includes major assignments that you may be asked to manage satisfactorily almost every day in your career.

The listing above makes no mention of the traditional duties of planning, organizing, and controlling. The computer complexities will also include directing as a major duty, one that crosses departmental lines of responsibility.

The size of an organization may dictate which duties and responsibilities will demand the greatest amount of attention. This in no way removes the installation manager from the responsibility of providing accurate and complete information. This especially holds true in the small shop where decisions are made quicker with fewer study committees and meetings.

Certain basic problems of DP management remain constant throughout every operation. Configurations and the number of employees in a shop may change almost constantly. Documentation provides for a continuity of operations in cases of high employee turnover rates, accidents, etc. Backup procedures are required to keep the installation operable in case of severe machine failure or some other disaster. Good management does not end with acquisition of certain technical skills. Managers of the very large shops may possess limited technical skills, but are deeply concerned in insuring the successful, continued operations of perhaps multiple-CPU installations. Just because your installation is considered to be small does not eliminate problems or reduce the need for basic management principles.

In any installation, there are always budget restrictions, whether the budget is formalized or not. These externally imposed limitations are more easily managed in the smaller shop. Top management and computer operations are usually separated physically and geographically by only a few walls and halls. There is less need for committees and meetings to reach decisions. Actions taken are quicker due to this proximity. Management is also extremely interested in verifying the efficacy of the original computer decision. This same interest will manifest itself in budgetary allowances to insure success. In establishing a need and justification for a professional, well-run operation, you are proving the worth of the shop. This becomes the groundwork for building a continuing reputation and standard of excellence.

There are many personal advantages derived from supervising a small shop. You have the chance to create the documentation deemed necessary to fit the situation. From original suggestion to revision and final implementation, you are deeply involved in the entire project. Success or failure is almost totally dependent upon your actions and decisions. In some of the larger installations, you may never have the privilege of creating a totally complete system. In the smaller office, you may have the sometimes trying responsibility for *all* systems. This makes for a frustrating, but rewarding, experience.

The operator-manager is presented with all of the problems facing a director of management information systems (MIS) for a large corporation. Dollar costs or rewards may differ, not the problems. When the work-load has increased sufficiently to allow a reasonable size staff, some managerial duties may be assigned to subordinates. Though spreading responsibilities across a wider base of personnel, the manager still retains ultimate responsibility. You will be called upon to make all operational decisions for the installation. There are positive aspects to enjoy in having total responsibility for data processing. This freedom includes the additional duty of making correct decisions. It is *your* shop—when you must accept responsibilities for errors and also accept praise for a job well-done.

Every situation is unique. Installations for the same industry with identical configurations are subject to varying degrees of management emphasis. One firm may be devoted to electronic recordkeeping; another may be more interested in production management. Regardless of your past background and experience, the installation in *this* company must be doubly receptive to management's requests for additional information and new applications. A computer installation exists to supply information for making decisions. Your future with the company will depend upon the contributions to profitability made through effective utilization of computer resources.

As you develop your skills in management, you are also building a reputation for excellence in the industry (DP). Technical skills or programming and management are quite easily transportable between firms and departments. Inside the company, you may be asked to assume additional duties, or reasonably be promoted to another department. On the outside, a firm may need to hire a bright, young manager to clean up the mess created by a less-than-professional manager.

These two examples present quite a dilemma. Simultaneously, this also proves the need for documentation, backup, and procedures. When your present employer asks you to assume responsibilities in another department, you must have all procedures in place so you can readily leave. If your availability is delayed while you document all procedures and train your replacement, the opportunity may be lost. In leaving an existing shop in a weakened condition for another shop that is already sickly and ailing, you may be stepping deeper into the mire of mismanagement. This will not enhance your reputation for management.

Recommended Reading

These books are included for general management interest and are only distantly related to data processing. They should be considered as an eclectic addition to your personal management information system.

1. Antony Jay, *Management and Machiavelli*. New York: Holt, Rinehart and Winston, 1968.
2. Alvin Toffler, *Future Shock*. New York: Random House, 1970.
3. Antony Jay, *Corporation Man*. New York: Randon House, 1971.
4. David Ogilvy, *Confessions of an Advertising Man*. New York: Atheneum, 1963.

Index